W9-AND-926

SPOTLIGHT

NEGRIL &
MONTEGO BAY

OLIVER HILL

Contents

NEGRIL &
MONTEGO BAY

NEGRIL AND THE WEST

Hanover and Westmoreland are Jamaica's westernmost parishes. Hanover wraps around from Montego Bay on its northeastern border to where Negril's large hotel strip overflows from Westmoreland at its western reaches. It's a picturesque parish with small mountains tapering down to the coast with rivers, lush valleys, and deep, navigable coves. Caves dot the landscape of some of Jamaica's most biologically diverse ecosystems, in the shadow of the Dolphin Head mountain range.

Negril, which straddles the Hanover–Westmoreland border, has become a mass-market destination popular among Jamaicans and foreign visitors alike. The Kingstonian phenomenon of a weekend escape to "country" often implies a trip west to kick back and adopt the beach life, which necessarily involves

taking in spectacular sunsets and the enviable slow pace evoked in Tyrone Taylor's 1983 hit, "Cottage in Negril." A constant stream of new visitors also gives hustlers a chance to do their thing, and Negril has gained a reputation as a mecca for sinful indulgence as a result.

While Negril is the region's most well-known draw, there are several low-key communities farther east that are just as easily accessible from Montego Bay's international airport and worthy coastal destinations in themselves, namely Little Bay, Bluefields, Belmont, and Whitehouse. The Westmoreland interior consists of vast alluvial plains on either side of Cabarita River, still some of Jamaica's most productive sugarcane territory. The plains extend from the base of the Orange Hill, just east of Negril, to where the Roaring River rises

© OLIVER HILL

HIGHLIGHTS

◖ Seven-Mile Beach: Seven-Mile Beach is great for long walks into the sunset (page 11).

◖ Royal Palm Reserve: Home to the Morass species of palm, found nowhere else, the reserve is also an important habitat for a slew of domestic and migratory birds (page 12).

◖ Dolphin Head Mountain: The small mountain range near Lucea claims some of Jamaica's highest rates of biodiversity and endemic species (page 40).

◖ Half Moon Beach: A languid horseshoe-shaped beach 15 minutes' drive east of Negril has fine sand and undeveloped coastline, reef, and islands (page 41).

◖ Roaring River and Blue Hole Garden: One of Jamaica's most picturesque blue holes sits in a lush garden near the source of Roaring River (page 43).

◖ Mayfield Falls: The best waterfalls attraction in Westmoreland, Mayfield is easily accessible and a good day's fun (page 43).

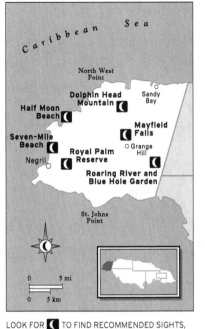

LOOK FOR ◖ TO FIND RECOMMENDED SIGHTS, ACTIVITIES, DINING, AND LODGING.

out of the earth from its underground source in the hills above Blue Hole Garden.

PLANNING YOUR TIME

Negril is the ultimate place to kick back on the beach and forget what day of the week it is. The general area has other worthwhile sights, however, which can help avoid sunburn and provide a glimpse of the "true" Jamaica—with all the allure of its countryside lifestyle and lush scenery. Most visitors to Negril come specifically to laze on the beach in the dead of winter, but there are special events throughout the year to be considered if you're planning a trip with some flexibility.

Negril is invaded each year March–April by

American college kids on all-inclusive spring break vacation packages. The spring breakers come from different institutions over the course of the month, but mostly during the first and second weeks of March. Recent years have been disappointing from an economic standpoint, with fewer visitors than years past. Still, you will want to keep this in mind when planning your trip to Negril—to either avoid the spring break crowd or coincide with it, depending on what you hope to get out of your beach vacation.

HISTORY

Negril's natural beauty has been appreciated for centuries, first by the Tainos, Jamaica's

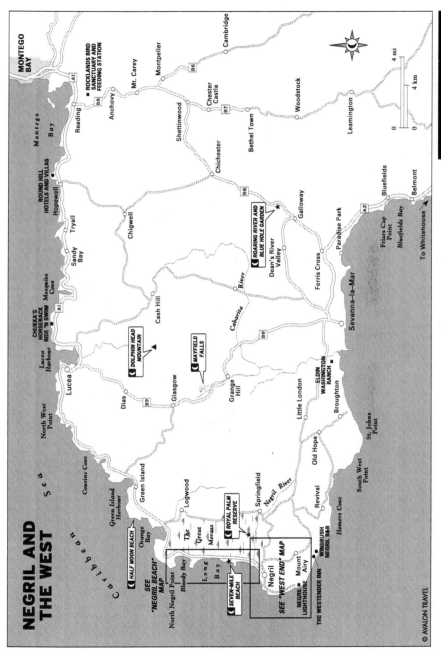

NEGRIL AND THE WEST

MONTEGO BAY

ROCKLANDS BIRD SANCTUARY AND FEEDING STATION

Cambridge

Montpelier

Mt. Carey

Anchovy

Reading

Montego Bay

ROUND HILL HOTELS AND VILLAS

Hopewell

Chigwell

Tryall

Sandy Bay

Mosquito Cove

CHUKKA'S HORSEBACK RIDE 'N SWIM

Lucea Harbour

North West Point

Lucea

Dias

Glasgow

Cousins Cove

Green Island Harbour

Green Island

Orange Bay

HALF MOON BEACH

SEE "NEGRIL BEACH" MAP

North Negril Point

Bloody Bay

Long Bay

SEVEN-MILE BEACH

Negril

NEGRIL LIGHTHOUSE

SEE "WEST END" MAP

THE WESTENDER INN

Caribbean Sea

Sea

Cash Hill

DOLPHIN HEAD MOUNTAIN

MAYFIELD FALLS

Grange Hill

Logwood

The Great Morass

ROYAL PALM RESERVE

Springfield

Negril River

Mount Airy

WINDRUSH NEGRIL B&B

Shettinwood

Chester Castle

Bethel Town

Woodstock

Leamington

Chichester

Galloway

ROARING RIVER AND BLUE HOLE GARDEN

Dean's River Valley

Cabarita River

Ferris Cross

ELDIN WASHINGTON RANCH

Little London

Broughton

Old Hope

Revival

South West Point

Homers Cove

St. Johns Point

Savanna-la-Mar

Paradise Park

Friars Cup Point

Bluefields Bay

Bluefields

Belmont

To Whitehouse

4 mi

4 km

A1

B8

B6

B7

B8

B9

A2

B9

© AVALON TRAVEL

first inhabitants; later by pirates and fishermen; and, finally, after a road was built connecting Negril to Green Island in 1959, by the rest of Jamaica and the world at large. Negril Harbor, or Bloody Bay as it is more commonly known, got its name from the whales slaughtered there, whose blood turned the water red. Today the water is crystal clear. The bay was a favorite hangout for the pirate Calico Jack Rackham and his consort piratesses Mary Read and Anne Bonney, all of whom were captured drunk and partying in Bloody Bay.

Calico Jack was hanged in Kingston, while his female counterparts were pardoned. Bloody Bay was also a regular departure point for ships heading to Europe, which would go in fleets to ensure their survival on the high seas. The Bay also provided a hiding place from which ambushes were launched on Spanish ships. It was also the departure point for the British naval mission, which saw 50 British ships launch a failed attempt to capture Louisiana, culminating in the Battle of New Orleans during the American War of Independence.

Negril

Negril has become Jamaica's foremost beach town, evolving over the past decade along with the changing nature of the tourists who come to bask in the sun and adopt the island's pace. Today, world-class restaurants and lodging provide an alternative to the low-key guesthouses and seafood stalls that became the norm during Negril's transition from fishing village to tourist boomtown in the 1970s. What was once Jamaica's secret paradise is today the heart of the island's diversified tourist economy.

Orientation

Life in Negril is focused on the west-facing coastline, which is divided between Seven-Mile Beach and the West End, or the Cliffs. Seven-Mile Beach runs from Bloody Bay in Hanover on its northern end to the mouth of the Negril River in Westmoreland, on the southern end of Long Bay. There are three principal roads that meet at the roundabout in the center of Negril: Norman Manley Boulevard, which turns into the A1 as it leaves town heading northeast toward Mobay; West End Road, which continues along the coast from the roundabout hugging the cliffs well past the lighthouse, until it eventually turns inland, rejoining the main south coast road (A2) in the community of Negril Spot; and Whitehall Road, which extends inland

from the roundabout toward the golf course, becoming the A2 at some point, with no warning before continuing on toward Sav-la-Mar.

Safety

Due to its status as Jamaica's foremost tourism mecca, Negril tends to attract some of the island's most aggressive hustlers. Many will feign friendship and generosity only to demand, often with aggression and intimidation, exorbitant compensation for whatever good or service is on offer, whether it's a CD of one of the countless "up-and-coming artists," a marijuana spliff handed to you as someone extends their hand in greeting, or a piece of jewelry. As a rule, do not accept anything you don't actually want, and clarify the expected compensation if you do want it before allowing anyone to put something in your hand or mouth. It is not uncommon for these kinds of hustlers to draw a knife to intimidate you, and there is generally little fear of repercussions from the police, who tend to be slow-moving if responsive at all. The police are unlikely to be sympathetic, especially if a quarrel or skirmish involves drugs, even if the mix-up was unprovoked. Do your best to stay in well-populated areas, and try to avoid unsolicited approaches from strangers offering something you don't want.

SIGHTS
Bloody Bay

Bloody Bay is located just north of the piece of land jutting out toward Booby Cay that is home to Hedonism II, Point Village, and Breezes Grand Negril. Bloody Bay is currently dominated by all-inclusive hotels, including two relatively new Riu hotels, SuperClub's flagship Breezes Grand Negril, Couples Negril, and the private beach for Sunset at the Palms, located across the road. The beach on Bloody Bay is accessible to nonguests at several points along the road, most easily at the **Office of Nature** (contact PR agent Joseph Reid, cell tel. 876/369-0395), which is just past the fenced-off private beach of Sunset at the Palms. Here you can chill out and get lobster and fish (11 A.M.–sunset, US$10–30) from the outdoor grill manned by Robert, Symore, and Binghi. Next door, Johnny P's Jamaican Kitchen (cell tel. 876/999-6325, US$2–3) serves up staples like chicken with rice and peas. On the same little stretch of beach, Ackee (Roydel Reid, cell tel. 876/868-7312) and Andy (Conrad Getten, cell tel. 876/894-3042) take visitors out for snorkeling excursions (1.5 hrs, US$20/person with two-person minimum) and glass-bottomed boat tours. The fish and lobster vendors at the Office of Nature tend to be quite aggressive in soliciting business, to the point of discomfort, and sadly the lobster and fish they extract from the sea get smaller and smaller with each passing year, throwing into question the ethical merit of supporting their business from an environmental standpoint.

◖ Seven-Mile Beach

Jamaica's longest beach is no longer the undisturbed keep of fishermen, as it was in the 1960s, but there are plenty of benefits that have come as a result of the virtually uncurbed development of the last 30 years. The sand remains a beautiful golden color, and the waters, while increasingly over-fished, remain crystal clear. A bar is never more than an arm's length away, and every kind of water sport is available. Expect advances from all manner of

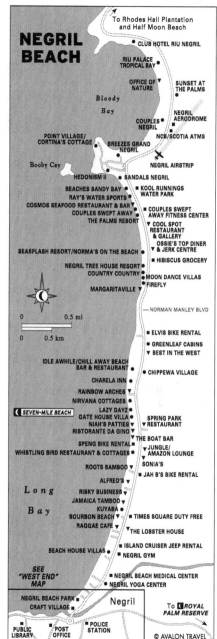

© OLIVER HILL

Seven-Mile Beach is what put Negril on the map as a favorite subdued hideaway for roving hippies in the 1970s.

peddler and hustler until your face becomes known and your reaction time to these calls for attention slows. The northern end of the beach is cordoned off by security in front of the all-inclusive resorts, while at the southern end the Negril River forms a natural border by the fishermen's village and crafts market. Also on the southern end is Negril's community park, where dances and daytime events are sometimes held.

☾ Royal Palm Reserve

Managed by the Negril Area Environmental Protection Trust (NEPT) and located 1.5 kilometers into the middle of the Great Morass from Sheffield, the 121-hectare Royal Palm Reserve (cell tel. 876/364-7407, nept_negril@yahoo, www.nept.wordpress.com, 9 A.M.–6 P.M. daily, US$15) is home to 114 plant species, including the endemic morass royal palms found only in western Jamaica. It's also home to over 300 animal species, including insects, reptiles (including two species of American crocodile), and birds.

The 26 resident bird species, which include the Jamaican woodpecker, Jamaican oriole, Jamaican euphonia, Jamaican parakeet, and the endemic endangered West Indian whistling duck, are joined by 16 migratory species that arrive at different times of the year. Admission includes a guided tour around 0.75 kilometers of boardwalk, and the ponds are open for sportfishing (US$5 with your own gear); you are almost guaranteed to catch African perch, tilapia, or tarpon. Shuttle service can be arranged (US$20 per person) from Negril. Royal Palm Reserve was leased by NEPT from the Petroleum Corporation of Jamaica (PCJ) as an alternative to a peat-mining project that had been planned. In the environmental impact study, it was found the project would have destroyed the beach and reef ecosystems. The present facilities were completed in 1989. Bird-watchers should make reservations with the NEPT office (tel. 876/957-3736) to get in earlier than normal opening hours. There is a nice bar area overlooking the water where drinks are served.

Other Sights

Whitehall Great House is yet another great house in ruins, located on the old Whitehall Estate on the ascent to Mount Airy. To get there, take a right immediately before the Texaco Station on Good Hope Road heading east from the Negril roundabout toward Sav-la-Mar. The ruins are about a mile up the hill on the left and command an excellent view of Negril Beach and the morass. One of the largest cotton trees in Jamaica stands on the property.

Bongo's Farm (tel. 876/880-7500, fanette@mail.infochan.com), owned by Bongo and Fanette Johnson, hosts visitors for hikes over gorgeous terrain with great views of Negril's coastline. This is the best place within 10 minutes of the beach to kick back and unwind in a truly Jamaican rural setting; the lush vegetation and laid-back company make for a great attraction. Jelly coconuts are

served fresh from the tree, and visitors are shown a variety of botanical specimens cultivated on the farm.

Negril Lighthouse is located near the westernmost point of Jamaica on West End Road just past The Caves. The lighthouse dates from 1894 and stands 30 meters above the sea.

ENTERTAINMENT

The great thing about Negril is the fact that no matter the season, you can forget what day of the week it is in a hurry. While weekends remain "going-out nights," and important acts that draw large Jamaican audiences will perform generally on a Friday or Saturday, big artists also perform on Monday, Wednesday, and Thursday nights. Because Negril is so small, the handful of clubs that monopolize the regular live entertainment market have made a tacit pact whereby each takes a night, or two, of the week. This way, the

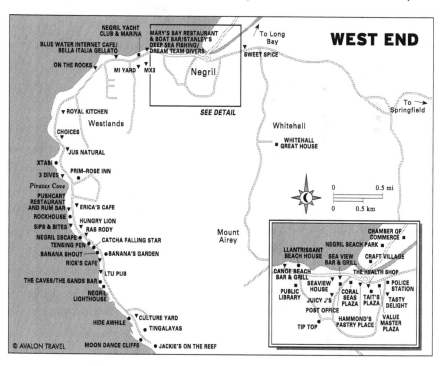

NEGRIL WEEKLY NIGHTLIFE SCHEDULE

Note that ranges in cover fees indicate the charges for a regular night with a local group versus a big-name act.

MONDAY
Live Reggae at Bourbon Beach (US$5-10)

TUESDAY
Live Reggae Beach Party at Alfred's (US$4)

WEDNESDAY
Live Music at Roots Bamboo (from US$5)

THURSDAY
Live Reggae at Bourbon Beach (US$5-10)

Ladies Night at The Jungle (US$7-9)

FRIDAY
Live Reggae Beach Party at Alfred's (US$4)

SATURDAY
Live Reggae at Bourbon Beach (US$5-10)
Party Night at The Jungle (US$7-9)
Saturday Night Live buffet at Seastar Inn (US$15)

SUNDAY
Jazz at Roots Bamboo (free)
Live Reggae Beach Party at Alfred's (US$4)

main clubs are guaranteed a weekly following, and Negril's transient crowd can somewhat keep tabs on where to go on any particular evening.

Bars and Clubs

Negril has an overwhelming number of bars and grills. This section covers establishments that are recommended more as nightlife draws, rather than for their food.

The Jungle (tel. 876/954-4005 or 876/954-4819, info@junglenegril.com, www.junglene-gril.com) is Negril's only off-the-water club, located in an old bank toward the middle of the beach on the morass side of Norman Manley Boulevard. It has regular theme nights throughout the week, as well as special events, normally held on weekends. Ladies' Night on Thursdays gets packed, and Saturdays generally see a good crowd dancing well into the morning. The Amazon Lounge at Jungle is open daily (4 P.M. to midnight).

Margaritaville (tel. 876/957-4467) has been headquarters for spring break activities for a number of years and is one of the most successful bar chains on the island. Villa Negril, as the Negril branch is called, is a more laid-back version of the Jimmy Buffet franchise than its Mobay or Ochi counterparts.

When it isn't peak party season, it's mostly known for its giveaways and beach parties on Tuesdays and Wednesdays in the early evening. Margaritaville is one of the venues frequently used for the Absolute Temptation Isle (ATI) events around Emancipation weekend.

Risky Business (tel. 876/957-3008) has live reggae three nights a week and is a bar and grill daily. Monday is Appleton's Ladies' Night, on Thursdays all local liquor is US$2. Saturday it's a bottomless mug 8 P.M.–1 A.M. (US$12).

Roots Bamboo Beach Resort (tel. 876/957-4479, rootsbamboobeach@hotmail.com) is run by the congenial Ted Plumber. It's been in business since 1979, when Ted bought the property and constructed bamboo bungalows. Ted was inspired by camping communities he saw along lakes in Canada. When Hurricane Gilbert destroyed the bungalows in 1988, he built the current concrete-and-wood houses. Care should be taken to secure your belongings, should you stay at Roots Bamboo. Security has been an issue in the past, as the bar hosts live music a few nights per week and nonguests take over the property. Roots Bamboo has been an entertainment venue since 1985 and recently started free live jazz 6–10 P.M. on Sundays, in addition to its long-standing live performances on Wednesdays.

© OLIVER HILL

The Jungle is Negril's longstanding club, with a busy schedule of guest selectors, parties, and performances througout the year.

Bourbon Beach (tel. 876/957-4405, www.bourbonbeachnegril.com, www.negrilreggae.com) took over from Debuss and is owned by four brothers and two sisters and managed by Jimmy Morrell. Monday Reggae Magic features internationally known acts like Gregory Isaacs, John Holt, and Yellowman, who are all regulars. Bourbon Thursdays features young and up-and-coming reggae acts and some of the more obscure local acts, and Saturdays Live on the Beach are usually reserved for a live local act, like Vybz Kartel or vintage artist like Ken Booth and The Mighty Diamonds. Bourbon Beach serves the best jerk on the beach from a pit on one side of the venue from mid-morning late into the night.

Alfred's Ocean Palace (tel. 876/957-4669, info@alfreds.com, www.alfreds.com) has been in operation since 1982. Jamaican and international cuisine with chicken, shrimp, and fish dishes (US$10–15) is served 8 A.M.–10:30 P.M. daily in high season; the kitchen closes at 9 P.M. in the low season. Alfred's also has eight double- and triple-occupancy rooms

(US$40–50). Sundays, Tuesdays, and Fridays are Live Reggae Beach Party nights, which typically feature local acts (US$4) with occasional big-name international acts like Toots and Capleton (US$10–15).

Jamaica Tamboo (tel. 876/957-4282,) is perhaps best known as the location for some of the parties during ATI weekend around Independence Day. Occasional events are held at other times throughout the year as well, while it functions day-to-day as a restaurant and sports bar. The beachfront property has basic rooms and wireless Internet at a good value (US$60).

MX3 (contact Clive "Kubba" Pringle, cell tel. 876/851-8831, actionparknegril@gmail.com) has been functioning as a party lawn since 1990 where occasional plays, stage shows and boxing matches are held. Email or call to find out what's upcoming. In 2010 Spiritz Nightclub opened at the lawn.

Sexy Rexy Sunset Cliff (between Rick's Cafe and The Caves, www.sexyrexynegril.com, cell tel. 876/445-3740, 10 A.M.–6 A.M. daily)

serves Jamaican and vegetarian dishes with a cliff-side bar ideal for taking in sunsets. Rexy Tomlinson established the joint in 1978.

Wavz (cell tel. 876/881-9289, www. wavzevents.com) is a seasonal venue and promotions company that hosts occasional parties throughout the year.

Negril Beach Park hosts Flava Sundays, drawing the biggest crowd in Negril on any given week with a nice mix of tourists, expats, and locals for dancehall sessions featuring top sound systems from Jamaica and abroad. Contact the park manager Clive "Kubba" Pringle (cell tel. 876/851-8831, actionparknegril@gmail.com) for more information.

On The Rocks (noon–midnight daily) is an interesting bar with what looks like a drive-in movie theater in its parking lot. Movies are played nightly (free admission), and popcorn and ice cream are served. Inexpensive drinks in a vibesy setting close to the water's edge make this a good place to down a mid-evening drink before hitting the clubs.

Festivals and Events

The weekends around Emancipation Day (August 1, 1838) and Independence Day (August 6, 1962) are filled with parties in Negril as **Absolute Temptation Isle** (www.ati-weekend.com) and competing event **Appleton Treasure Island** (contact Appleton's Kingston office, tel. 876/923-6141, appleton@infochan. com) try to outdo each other by throwing the hottest and most frequent parties. Big-time promoters from Kingston and Miami draw Jamaica's party youth from across the globe, who arrive to indulge in booze, ganja, general debauchery, and a few stage shows. ATI Weekend is well worthwhile as a more genuinely Jamaican party scene and it's the only

NEGRIL'S EMANCIPATION-INDEPENDENCE PARTIES

Every summer at the end of July, masses of Jamaican youth descend on Negril and book virtually every room in town for what's known as ATI Weekend (www.atiweekend.com), or simply ATI. All-inclusive parties go virtually non-stop for three or four days straight. ATI stands for Absolute Temptation Isle, but in 2006, Appleton's Rum, a sponsor in previous years, formed its own competing ATI the following weekend – adopting the same acronym, which in this case stands for Appleton Treasure Island.

The original ATI, organized by Alex Chin, promoter and founder of Absolute Entertainment, began in Negril in 2000 as Stages, bringing to Jamaica a regular party held in Miami a few times per year. The idea was to replicate the mood of Trinidad's or Brazil's Carnival, with crowds moving from party to party for days on end. The event has grown steadily with several promoters coming together each year to organize different parties at venues around Negril that include Wavz, Tamboo, Margaritaville, and Chances, each with a different theme – from foam parties to

stage shows. A host of selectors are brought in, as well as many of Jamaica's most popular contemporary dancehall artists. Selectors often include Black Chiney from Miami, Xcaliber from Trinidad, Jamaica's top sound, Renaissance, and DJ Chrome from Zip FM. There is no better week to be in Negril for those seeking an overwhelming dose of booze, flesh, and sound.

Even though Appleton's pulled its sponsorship of the original ATI, other sponsors stepped in readily. The Jamaica Tourist Board also endorsed the event for the first time in 2006. Appleton's competing event now bookends the festivities held to coincide with Jamaica's Emancipation and Independence celebrations. Spring break pales in comparison.

All-inclusive parties in Jamaica have been around since the early 1990s, when the famous Frenchman's Parties, organized by Ian Wong as Jamaica's most exclusive regular all-inclusive soiree, began. Frenchman's parties are held a few times annually, the main "sell-off" events being staged for New Year's and Heroes Weekend.

time of year when Negril is decidedly taken over by Jamaicans, making spring break look like child's play.

The **Reggae Marathon, Half Marathon, and 10K** (contact director Alfred "Frano" Francis, tel. 876/922-8677, racedirector@ reggaemarathon.com, or marketing director Diane Ellis, frandan@cwjamaica.com, www. reggaemarathon.com) held at the beginning of December, is a popular event drawing locals, expats, and runners from abroad for a race on a mostly flat, IAAF-certified route starting at Long Bay Beach Park on Seven-Mile Beach, going into the town of Negril, and heading north toward the town of Green Island before looping to the finish line back at Long Bay Beach Park. Events start on Friday with registration, a pasta party, and village bash. Races start at the crack of dawn on Saturday, with a ceremony later in the day where winners compete for a total purse of over US$10,000 in prize money. You must be 18 years old to run the marathon, and at least age 10 for the 10K.

Fees are US$85 per person for the marathon and US$60 for the 10K on or before July 31, US$95 for marathon and US$70 for 10K after August 1.

The **Negril Jerk Festival** (contact 3 Dives Jerk Centre owner Lyndon Myrie, a.k.a. Lloydie, tel. 876/957-0845 or 876/782-9990) is held on the last Sunday of November, where different jerk vendors from across the island are invited to set up stalls by 3 Dives Jerk Centre on the West End.

Miami Linkup (contact Robert "Dozer" Williams, cell tel. 954/479-0202 or 876/815-2198, rebeltsound@gmail.com, www.rebeltsound.com), an event promotions group, hosts an annual Spring Break party that draws large crowds to a stage show brimming with the hottest of Jamaica's dancehall and reggae artists around the second weekend in March.

Western Consciousness (contact promoter Worrel King, cell tel. 876/383-7717 or 876/849-8426, kingofkingspro@hotmail.com, www.westernconsciousness.com) is a not-to-be-

Branzo stands in front of One Stop Branzo Wood Sculptures, where he carves away the days beachside.

missed reggae show for fans of conscious roots music put on by King of Kings Promotions in late April or May each year at Paradise Park on the outskirts of Savanna-la-Mar.

SHOPPING

Natural Vibes Souvenir Shop (between Jamaica Tamboo and Risky Business, tel. 876/352-5849, naturalvibesjamaica@gmail.com, 8 A.M.–7 P.M. daily) has been run by Haresh "Hassle Free Harry" Pahilwani since 2004 and is known for hassle-free shopping for Cuban cigars, Jamaica T-shirts and sweats, sandals, sunglasses, Rasta hats, and smoking paraphernalia.

Bongo Johnson (tel. 876/486-0006) makes beautiful art sculptures, which can be seen by special arrangement. Johnson's delicate lignum vitae sculptures are on exhibit at the National Gallery in Kingston. He could be convinced to sell a piece if the price is right.

Abdel, a.k.a. Branzo (cell tel. 876/867-4246), can be found in his **One Stop Branzo Wood Sculptures** shop on the beachfront at Wavz Entertainment Centre (8 A.M.–8 P.M. daily). Branzo is one of the most talented wood carvers around and also sells the work of several other woodworkers in his little shop.

Errol Allen (cell tel. 876/385-5399) is a talented local artist who makes unique silhouette sculptures and oil paintings. Allen's sculptures can be seen on the grounds of Whistling Bird.

CY Clothing, the best in Jamaican roots wear, can be found at **Tesori's** and **Joy's Boutique.**

Mary Wonson's Flower Hill Oil and Soap Company produces natural products like lip balms, soaps, rejuvenating oils, and restorative hair oil from extra virgin coconut oil. Contact Nordia Hill (cell tel. 876/358-9732) to see which retailers in the area are currently carrying the products or to place a direct order.

Chances Gift Shop and Cigar Hut (on beach next to Chances, tel. 876/957-3177) has all the Cubans you could smuggle home in your suitcase (or—less risky—enjoy while in Jamaica). Manager Martin is a pleasant chap and not overly pushy. The air-conditioning and smell of fresh tobacco is a good reason to stop in and browse.

Negril Crafts Market (between the Negril Beach Park and the river) has a wide variety of crafts, some better and more authentic than others. Sadly, an increasing proportion of the products on sale are made in China rather than locally produced.

Rutland Point Craft Centre is located next to the aerodrome just before the Petcom gas station, heading northeast toward Mobay.

A Fi Wi Plaza, next to Scotia Bank by the roundabout, has crafts and T-shirts from Sun Island.

Time Square Mall Plaza (tel. 876/957-9263, 9–7 P.M. daily, duty-free closed on Sun.) is located on Norman Manley Boulevard across from Bourbon Beach. The duty-free shopping center has several shops selling jewelry, Cuban cigars, crafts, liquor, watches, and trinkets.

Kosmic Gift Shop & Boutique (located next to Cosmos on the beach, Norman Manley Blvd., tel. 876/957-3940) has a mix of Rasta knit hats and "Jamaica, No problem" T-shirts.

SPORTS AND RECREATION

Opportunities for outdoor recreation are everywhere in Negril, from hiking to windsurfing and scuba diving.

Motor Bikes and Car Rentals

Speng Bike Rental (across from Jungle next to Westlea Cabins, tel. 876/414-5189) rents scooters (US$40) and dirt bikes (US$50), negotiable for multiple-day rental. Proprietor Tony Hilton also does airport transfers (US$60), as well as private tours.

Elvis Bike Rental (in front of Coco la Palm, tel. 876/848-9081) rents scooters (US$30/day, $140/week), a Honda shadow 600cc (US$50/day US$280/week), dirt bikes (US$40/day, US $210/week) as well as a Toyota Corolla (US$60/day, US$250/week).

Jah B's Bike Rentals (tel. 876/957-4235 or 876/353-9533, 8 A.M.–6 P.M. daily) rents 125cc Honda and Suzuki Scooters (US$35) and a 60cc Honda Shadow (US$50). The sign on the road says JB Bike Rental.

Tykes Bike Rental (West End Rd. across

from Tensing Pen, just before Rick's Cafe, tel. 876/957-0388, tonyvassell@yahoo.com, 8 A.M.–6 P.M. daily) rents 125cc scooters (US$45) and 175cc dirt bikes (US$50).

Island Cruiser Rentals (contact Patrick Marzouca, tel. 876/618-1277, cell tel. 876/422-2831 or 876/298-5400, info@islandcruiserjamaica.com, www.islandcruiserjamaica.com) rents a selection of brightly colored cruising vehicles for US$50 per day or US$325 per week.

Water Sports

Negril is overflowing with water sports opportunities. From excursions in glass-bottomed boats to parasailing, riding personal watercraft, windsurfing, scuba, snorkeling, and catamaran cruises, there is something for every level of enthusiasm and interest.

Dream Team Divers (Mary's Bay, tel. 876/957-0054 or 876/831-0435, info@dreamteamdiversjamaica.com, www.dreamteamdiversjamaica.com, 8 A.M.–4 P.M. daily) has English, German, Italian, and French-speaking dive instructors. Dive master Ken Brown has run every dive shop in town since he landed in Negril in 1991 and finally opened his own shop in October 2008. Dream Team offers free pickup and drop-off for clients from any accommodation in Negril. The outfit sets itself apart by visiting dolphin dive sites and locations not visited by any others. Rates range from the Discover Scuba intro course (US$80) to the dive master certification (US$600).

Negril Scuba Centre (neg.scuba.centre@cwjamaica.com, www.negrilscuba.com) has three locations, Negril Escape (tel. 876/957-4425), Mariner's (876/957-4425), and Negril Beach Village (tel. 876/957-0392) on Bloody Bay Beach across Norman Manley Boulevard from Sunset at The Palms. The scuba center offers dive packages that include accommodations at Negril Escape and Spa, where the center is based, or at other participating hotels. Popular dive sites include Booby Cay Island, The Arches, Ballard's Reef, a Deep Plane, Gallery, King Fish Point, the Throne Room and Blue Castle Ship Wreck, among several others. PADI courses range from a beginner three-hour Discover

Diving session (US$80) to Advanced Open Water (US$300), Rescue Diver (US$350), and Scuba Master (US$600) courses. Those already certified can rent tanks (US$40) and shortie wetsuits (US$6/day). Several other water sports activities are offered besides.

Ray's Water Sports (tel. 876/957-5349, info@rayswatersportsnegril.com, www.rayswatersportsnegril.com) is one of the more successful outfits on the beach, impossible to miss with his name.

Negril Treehouse has a water sports center managed by Ron Mirey, which offers parasailing (US$40), Jet Skis (US$50/half hour) and fishing trips (US$150 up to four people).

Aqua Nova Water Sports (Mariners Beach Club, tel. 876/957-4323 or 876/957-4754) offers Jet Skis (by Coral Seas) and parasailing (US$50/person or US$80/couple) from its office at Mariners Negril Beach Club. Aqua Nova also runs regular three-hour catamaran and trimaran cruises, one leaving at 10:30 A.M. (US$60 includes lunch and open bar), the other at 3:30 P.M. (US$50 includes snack and open bar). Boats pick up guests from hotels along the beach. Private charters are also offered for US$250 for three hours.

Kool Runnings (tel. 876/957-5400, info@koolrunnings.com, 11 A.M.–6 P.M. Wed., Sat., and Sun. in low season, 9 A.M.–5 P.M. daily in high season, US$28 adults/over four feet, US$19 children under four feet tall, two years and under free) is a water park with several slides and a lazy river for gentle tubing. It's located across from Beaches Sandy Bay. There is food and a bar on the property, as well as a juice bar and coffee shop. With a 2,500-person capacity, the water park regularly hosts events, including wild parties during Emancipation-Independence celebrations in early August. A stage provides live entertainment, with reggae pumping throughout the day.

Kool Runnings' Kool Kanoe Swamp Adventure Tour takes visitors on a guided tour of the Great Morass, Jamaica's largest wetland area, located in the water park's back yard. Visitors ride on an inflatable "kanoe" to paddle along a guided tour through the canals of the morass to see some of the plants and animals in their natural habitat. Those favoring a more independent experience can use kayaks to guide themselves through the morass. You are likely to encounter yellow snakes, land crabs, mongoose, turtles, and birds. The water park holds a Soldier Crab Derby, allowing visitors to bet on the winners.

Three restaurants on property serve Jamaican dishes, while the Kool Blendz juice bar serves natural smoothies.

Golf

Negril Hills Golf Club (Sheffield, east of the roundabout on the A2, tel. 876/957-4638, www.negrilhillsgolfclub.com, 7:30 A.M.–3 P.M.) has reasonable rates for nonmembers. For 9 holes: greens fee (US$28.75), cart (US$17.25), caddy (US$7); for 18 holes: greens fee (US$57.50), cart (US$34.50), caddy (US$14). Clubs can also be rented (US$18 for older, US$25 for newer, and US$40 for top-of-the-line and Hybrid clubs (e.g. Taylor Made and Cobras).

Horseback Riding

Wild Crocodile Adventures & Tours (contact Paul Washington, cell tel. 876/881-6917, wildcrocodile@hotmail.com, www.wildcrocodileadventures.com, US$60 per adult, US$45 children under 10, including transportation from Negril) based at Eldin Washington Ranch on the main road from Negril to Savanna-la-Mar, features horseback riding on a 900-acre farm populated by a variety of animals from peacocks to ostriches, donkeys, and goats. There are three riding times daily: 9 A.M., noon, and 3 P.M. There's no minimum group size. The 2.5-hour ride ends on a one-mile stretch of private beach.

Paradise Park (tel. 876/955-2675, paradise1@cwjamaica.com, US$40 per person) is one of the best places in Jamaica for down-to-earth small-group rides on an expansive seaside ranch a few kilometers east of Savanna-la-Mar in Ferris Cross. Groups of up to 10 riders are led through beautiful countryside to a river park and private beach for a 1.5-hour ride. The cost of the ride includes a complimentary soft drink. Lunch can be arranged for groups of at least six with a 24-hour reservation (additional US$12 per person).

Chukka's Horseback Ride 'N Swim (tel. 876/953-5619, montegobay@chukkacaribbean.com, US$73) offers 2.5-hour rides through forest and along the shoreline before swimming on horseback. Remember to bring a change of clothes, and a waterproof camera if you don't want to buy photos from Chukka. The tour is located between Negril and Mobay, about a half hour to Negril and 40 minutes to Mobay in the fishing village of Sandy Bay. Chukka offers a two-hour dune buggy excursion for people over 18 ($76) and two-hour ATV tours ($75). Canopy ziplines, tubing, and kayaking are staged from the Montpelier Chukka location.

Rhodes Hall Plantation (tel. 876/431-6322 or 876/957-6422, rhodesresort@comcast.net, www.rhodesresort.com) also has good horseback riding with an expansive seaside property five minutes northeast of Negril heading toward Montego Bay.

Fishing

The waters just off Negril's shoreline are severely over-fished, with very low counts found in surveys conducted by the Negril Area Environmental Protection Trust. Nevertheless, a bit farther offshore in deeper waters it's possible to catch plenty of wahoo and even marlin.

Stanley's Deep Sea Fishing (www.stanleysdeepseafishing.com, tel. 876/957-6341) is the most professional outfit in Negril. It's run by Captain Stanley Carvalho and offers a good mix of options from half-day (US$500) to three-quarter day (US$750) to full-day trips (US$1000) for up to four people. Additional persons can be added, up to eight passengers (additional person US$50/75/100 for the different length excursions). Stanley's also offers the option of charter sharing, where individuals can team up with others to fill up the boat (US$100) rather than charter exclusively.

Fitness Centers

Couples Swept Away (7:30 A.M.–9 P.M. daily)

has the best sports complex in Negril and offers a day pass (US$20/per person), which includes access to tennis, squash, and racquetball courts, a sauna, steam room, whirlpool tub, and a lap pool. Rackets are available for rent (US$10 each). Yoga and Pilates classes are offered daily at no extra charge. Tennis clinics are also included (Mon.–Fri.), but private lessons incur an additional charge.

Negril Fitness Centre (US$5/day, US$25/week, US$45/month) next to the Café Taino, has basic equipment like dumbbells, Stairmasters, and treadmills and serves a mostly Jamaican clientele.

Yoga and Massage

Fanette Johnson (cell tel. 876/897-9492, fanette@mail.infochan.com) leads Iyengar-style yoga sessions at Tensing Pen and Rockhouse and will also do private sessions. She has 20 years' experience teaching yoga around the globe.

Oya Oezcan (cell tel. 876/440-7071) offers therapeutic body massage.

Jackie's on the Reef (tel. 876/957-4997 or 718/469-2785, jackiesonthereef@rcn.com, www.jackiesonthereef.com) accepts nonguests for daily yoga sessions.

ACCOMMODATIONS
Seven-Mile Beach

Negril definitely has something for everyone when it comes to finding the ideal place to stay. From couples-only, all-inclusive resorts, to hip, inexpensive independent cottages by the sea and exclusive villas, there's an option for every taste and budget. Low-season and high-season rates apply here as much as, if not more than, the other tourism centers on the island. Some establishments increase rates in the middle of the low season for special events like Independence weekend at the beginning of August, when Jamaicans from "yard" and "abroad" flock for a torrent of nonstop parties that last for days on end.

Accommodations and food have been divided geographically by Negril's roundabout, which is used to distinguish between the properties on either side of Norman Manley Boulevard from those on the either side of West End Road. Within each price category, the accommodations are organized from north to south.

Seven-Mile Beach starts at the mouth of Negril River and stretches the length of Long Bay as well as Bloody Bay farther north. Long Bay is fronted by a multitude of small hotels as well as large all-inclusive resorts on its northern end.

UNDER US$100

Cortina's Cottage (cell tel. 876/382-6384, www.carolynscaribbeancottages.com, US$75) is actually a studio apartment located in the Point Village complex at the end of Seven-Mile Beach. It's a good option for those looking for all the amenities normally associated with a large resort at an affordable price. Swimming pool access, a private beach reserved for Point Village, make Cortina's an excellent option on the beach. The apartment is tastefully decorated with plenty of curtains.

Chippewa Village (tel. 876/957-4676, cell 876/885-7676, toll-free from US and Canada, 877-670-8426 or tel. 213/291-8382, chippewavillage@hotmail.com, www.chippewavillageresort.com) is a comfortable assortment of seven cottages on the morass side of Norman Manley Boulevard tastefully decorated with a Sioux motif. Owner John Babcook is a leather designer whose great-grandfather Red Shirt was chief of the Dakota Sioux and represented his nation at the 1906 World's Fair. Trails cut a quarter mile into the morass lead to a 16-foot viewing platform that affords an incredible 360-degree view of Negril, the morass, and the surrounding hills. In mid-2010 an open-air home theater was built under a canvass teepee in keeping with John's modernistic interpretation of Chippewa style.

Greenleaf Cabins (next to Chippewa Village on the morass side of Norman Manley Blvd., contact Marni, cell tel. 617/448-5180, info@indikanegril.com, www.indikanegril.com) has a spacious four-bedroom main building called Devon House, which sleeps up to seven people, and a next large structure with three bedrooms called Dolton House, which also sleeps seven (US$150 each building). Also on the property is a self-contained cottage with a full kitchen and two beds (US$60), as well as two rustic cabins (US$35), each with two beds, a small fridge, shower, and floor fan. The Dolton House bedrooms all have exterior entrances and can rent separately (US$50) and share the kitchen and living area. Airport transfers are offered with Devon (US$110 round-trip).

Firefly (tel. 876/9574358, tel. 8769579325, firefly@jamaicalink.com, www.jamaicalink. com, US$60–96 d) offers a range of accommodations from studio apartments to beachfront penthouse suites, in a garden setting with an assortment of cottages and rooms in a multi-story building.

Negril Yoga Centre (tel. 876/957-4397, negrilyoga@cwjamaica.com, www.negrilyoga. com, US$30–75), also known as The Little Oasis, has simple, clean, and nicely decorated rooms with single and double beds. The center is tasteful and secure, with a very good restaurant that specializes in vegetarian curries and Thai food cooked to order. The property boasts, "There is no bar, no pool, and no dance club at the Centre which keeps our prices low, and our ambience low-key."

Westport Cottages and Youth Hostel (tel. 876/957-4736, www.negrilwestportcottages. com, US$20–45) is a favorite budget accommodation, centrally located along Norman Manley Boulevard across from the beach, run by Joseph Matthews and Sister. The rustic wooden cottages have not increased their rates in decades, with simple double beds, standing fans, and use of the common kitchen, while the newer concrete buildings have virtually the same amenities at the higher rate. Joseph does airport pickups at reasonable cost.

US$100-250

Kuyaba (tel. 876/957-4318 or 876/957-9815, kuyaba@cwjamaica.com, www.kuyaba.com) is one of the longest-standing rental options on the beach and has developed into a handful of tasteful cottages. The more rustic cottages

© OLIVER HILL

the view from a raised thatch-roofed dining cabana at Kuyaba

(US$56–64 low, US$70–77 high season) hold true to Negril's original rustic hippie vibe, while newer, more elegant cottages (US$77–85 low, US$97–106 high season) have been added in recent years to round out the mix. All cottages have ceiling fans, air-conditioning, and private baths with hot water. A restaurant on the property has good food.

Rooms Negril (tel. 876/957-3500, toll-free from U.S. or Jamaica 877/467-8737, info@superclubs.com, www.superclubs.com, US$115–143 d) has basic garden view and oceanfront rooms with air-conditioning, cable TV, phones, and either one king-size or two double beds. Rates include continental breakfast.

Charela Inn (tel. 876/957-4277, fax 876/957-4414, info@charela.com, www.charela.com, US$126–183 d low season, US$189–194 d high season) is a medium-size hacienda-style property with deluxe suites facing the beach, as well as more humble garden-view rooms. Charela is one of the more tasteful large properties on Seven-Mile Beach, with well-designed and lushly planted grounds.

Seasplash Resort (tel. 876/957-4041, seasplash@cwjamaica.com, www.seasplash.com, US$96/146 low/high season) is a large concrete structure with little to distinguish it from many other similar hotels that crowd Seven-Mile Beach. The suites are nonetheless spacious, clean, and well appointed with complete amenities. It's also home to Norma's on the Beach.

⟨ Whistling Bird Restaurant & Cottages (tel. 876/957-4403, or from the U.S. toll-free 800/276-8054, whistlingbird@negriljamaica.com, www.whistlingbird.com, from US$98/140 low/high season) has been operated by proprietor Jim Boydston since 1978, when Negril's tourism boom was in its infancy. The property consists of 12 cottages with a total of 20 rooms spread over lush tropical gardens. The rainforest-like setting attracts many birds, including Jamaica's national bird, the red-billed streamertail. The cottages have simple, tasteful rooms with an open layout, the larger ones villa-sized at 4–6 rooms. Half the rooms have air-conditioning, with TV available on request. Whistling Bird has an excellent restaurant that prides itself on its "fancy Jamaican" cooking, offering five-course gourmet dinners (US$35). A variety of packages are available, with a significant proportion of guests opting for the all-inclusive option at US$125–189 per person daily. Whistling Bird is a popular setting for weddings, retreats, and corporate meetings.

The Palms Resort (tel. 876/957-4375, info@thepalmsnegril.com, www.thepalmsnegril.com, US$113/120 low/high season) previously Paradise View, has been undergoing a process of complete transformation under the new ownership of the Nelson family. Wooden furniture, louvered windows, and sleek styling throughout have added a modern, classy mood to the once-tired complex. Kristyl's restaurant on the beach is set poolside on a wooden deck with plush furniture. Wireless Internet reaches the rooms and pool/bar area, and guests are provided a computer in the office. Rooms have queen- or king-size beds, private baths with hot water, private balconies, and cable TV. Most of the rooms are garden view, with a few seaview deluxe rooms (US$210/237 low/high season).

⟨ Country Country (tel. 876/957-4273, countrynegril@gmail.com, www.countryjamaica.com, US$140–155 low season, US$170–190 high season) has 17 cottages on the beach side of Norman Manley Boulevard, and three self-contained apartments on the morass side. Built in 2000, the cottages are well laid out in a lush garden setting that promotes quiet and privacy. Rooms have the same amenities throughout, namely air-conditioning, flat panel TVs with cable, spacious private baths with hot water, and porches. The superior and premium categories relate to the proximity to the beach. An expansion into the adjacent lot for a total of 50 units is in the works. Rates include breakfast, and Wi-Fi is available in the communal lounge by the office.

Negril Tree House Resort (tel. 876/957-4287, info@negril-treehouse.com, www.negril-treehouse.com, US$100–200 low, US$145–340 high season) has reasonable rates that vary depending on the size of the room and the view out the window (garden or sea). Manager Gail Jackson and her husband Jimmy Jackson had the first two buildings built in 1982 and have expanded the property successively to its current 70 units. Most rooms have king-size beds or two twins. Wireless Internet is available in the lobby and beach areas. There is also a water sports shop on the property. Jimmy Jackson runs Negril Spot Farm, which provides all the meat served at Negril Tree House. He was named farmer of the year in 2005 and 2006. Negril Tree House is moving toward 100 percent solar-powered hot water, with 25 percent of the hot-water systems already converted to solar.

Our Pastime Villas (tel. 876/957-5422 or U.S. tel. 636/448-8185, info@ourpasttimenegril.com, www.ourpasttimenegril.com) offers unpretentious deluxe rooms, studios, and two-bedroom apartments (US$60–250).

OVER US$250

⟨ Idle Awhile Resort (tel. 876/957-3303, U.S tel. 877/243-5352, fax 876/957-9567, stay@idleawhile.com, www.idleawhile.com, from US$130–200 low season, US$210–270 high season) opened in 1999, immediately establishing itself as one of the finest properties on Seven-Mile Beach. The rooms are beautifully decorated with louvered windows, minimalist designs, wooden furniture, ceiling fans, and air-conditioning. Idle Awhile guest have access to Negril's best sports complex at Couples Swept Away. Wireless Internet is included. An excellent restaurant, Chill Awhile, faces the beach, serving Jamaican and continental cuisine and fresh juices.

Aqua Negril Resort (tel. 876/957-9037 or cell tel. 876/417-1237, aquanegril@gmail.com, www.aquanegril.com, US$250–425) is a five-room high-end boutique resort with luxurious amenities run by Trini-Jamaican couple Ken and Liz Sealey. Rooms have king beds, air-conditioning, en suite baths, minifridges, flat panel TVs, and iPod docks. Wi-Fi is complimentary in the common area on the ground floor, and a computer terminal is available for those not carrying laptops. Prices include a complete breakfast. A Jacuzzi on the deck upstairs overlooks the sea and beach bar. The bar is open to the public and offers over 70 types of rum and countless cocktail concoctions.

Beach House Villas (tel. 876/957-4731, U.S. tel. 801/363-3529, contact@negriljamaicavillas.com, www.negril-hotels.com, from US$200/250 low/high season) has an assortment of self-contained units, which are well maintained and clean and command good views of the sea. All rooms have air-conditioning, TV, and hot water. The property has a total of 21 bedrooms for a maximum of 62 guests. An Internet connection is available in the common living area.

VILLAS

Gate House Villa (call Ali Provines to book, U.S. tel. 435/615-7474 or 888/595-1579, info@gatehousevilla.com, www.gatehousevilla.com) is a comfortable and stylish house with four rooms and a fully equipped kitchen. This is an ideal place for a medium-size group of up to eight people. The rooms, each with one king-size or two twin beds, rent individually for rates ranging US$89–109 in

low season, and US$139–159 in high season. (The most-expensive room is the large upstairs suite, which has a veranda overlooking the sea and a large open shower.) There is a bar, Tony's Hut, on the property, right on the beach. The whole property can also be rented (US$400/550 low/high season) and can sleep up to 10 people.

Moon Dance Villas (U.S. tel. 800/621-1120, info@moondancevillas.com) has an assortment of one- to five-bedroom villas (US$600–1,500 low season, US$700–1,900 high season) and is centrally located, with 300 feet of private sand on Seven-Mile Beach. Moon Dance rates include a chef, bartender, housekeeper, security, Internet, private pool and Jacuzzi, and airport transfer, with an unlimited food option (add US$115 per person daily). Moon Dance is an ideal accommodation option for families and small groups. A four-night minimum stay is required.

ALL-INCLUSIVE RESORTS

⟨ Sunset at the Palms (resort tel. 876/957-5350, reservations tel. 876/979-8870, or U.S. tel. 800/234-1707, www.sunsetatthepalms.com) is the most alluring of the Sunset Resorts' all-inclusive properties. It features small one-bedroom bungalows spread out across lush, well-manicured grounds. The food, with a mix of buffet style and à la carte meals, is markedly better than at the other Sunset properties, as is the level of service; prices are accordingly higher: US$350/545 low/high season per couple for a deluxe bungalow (US$75 extra per child), and US$540/742 low/high season for the one-bedroom suite.

Inside the bungalow-style cottages, a pleasant natural design with wooden furniture, Bali-esque detailing, and plush bedding are overwhelmingly inviting. The bathrooms are sleek and modern, with shower fixtures suitable for two.

Sunset at the Palms is set back from the beach across Norman Manley Boulevard, with a private beach right in the middle of Bloody Bay, a two-minute walk from the lobby. There's a bar and grill on the beach and water sports equipment. A tennis court and weight room are located across the road, as is a beautiful whirlpool tub and pool with a swim-up bar. Internet is available off the lobby.

Breezes Grand Negril (www.superclubs.com, US$224/389 low/high season), formerly Grand Lido Negril, is the flagship SuperClubs resort. One of the first SuperClubs properties, Breezes Negril has a dramatic entrance corridor surrounded by fountains and reflecting pools that lead into the lobby and dining areas. Breezes Negril has 210 junior and full suites, each equipped with full amenities including air-conditioning, satellite TV, direct-dial telephones, and CD player.

Several restaurants on the property give guests a lot of options. Piacere serves Nouvelle French–inspired cuisine in an elegant candlelit setting that requires formal attire (jackets, slacks, and shoes for men). Cafe Lido serves continental cuisine and is a bit more toned down on the dress-code, with a no-shorts rule. La Pasta is a more casual, Italian-inspired pasta bar open 3–10 P.M. daily. Breakfast and lunch are served at Gran Terraza, the open-air buffet area between the beach and the lobby; dinner is also served there 7:30–10 P.M. on Monday and Friday evenings. RASTAurant serves Jamaican favorites like jerk chicken and roti. Munasan is the newest restaurant on the property, serving authentic sushi and teppanyaki. The specialty restaurants are open 6:30–9:30 P.M. except Monday and Friday, and reservations may be required. Guests from other hotels may purchase a pass in order to dine at the restaurants (day pass US$79 per person, evening pass US$99 per person).

Breezes occupies the choice property on Bloody Bay, where calm inviting waters gently lap the shore. There is an *au natural* beach on one end of the property, with the main expanse of beach open to those who can keep their bathing suit on. The highlight of the nine-hectare gardens is a centuries-old cotton tree that stands between the 24-hour bar and the spa.

Couples has two properties in Negril: Couples Negril (tel. 876/957-5960, U.S. tel. 800/COUPLES, US$408/590 low/high season per couple per night), which is actually just across the border into Hanover, and Couples Swept Away (tel. 876/957-4061, US$413/602 low/high season per couple per night), at the north end of Long Bay. For proximity to offsite activities and an easy walk to Negril's nightlife, Couples Swept Away has clear advantages. On the other hand, for couples looking to get away from it all, including adjacent public beaches and other reminders of the existence of outside civilization, Couples Negril could be a better option.

Couples Swept Away is an exceptional all-inclusive with a new wing on the south end of the compound that has a wet bar, grill, and beautiful lounge tastefully decorated by Jane Issa, wife of Couples owner Lee Issa. Mr. Issa can often be found around the property, checking in with his guests and making sure everything is running smoothly. The gym facilities and tennis courts at Couples are top-notch. Day passes, offered for eight-hour periods (US$75), entitle pass-holders complete access to everything on the property.

Hedonism II (tel. 876/957-5200, www.superclubs.com, US$135–215 low season, US$175–285 high season) is the original and notorious all-inclusive resort where anything goes. Situated at the northern end of Negril's Long Bay, Hedonism II has 280 rooms and 15 suites, all with tiled floors, air-conditioning, TV, and, of course, mirrored ceilings. Many of the suites have private whirlpool tubs right on the beach. It's a great place for couples and singles looking to unwind and let go, and potentially do things they would never do at home—or alternatively, do exactly what's done at home whenever, wherever, and with whomever they see fit. Repeat guests don't keep going back for the food, but for the sexually charged atmosphere.

Two private beaches (one nude, one not) offer plenty of activities from water sports to volleyball to acrobatics. The main terrace dining area is complemented by Italian-inspired Pastafari, Japanese-inspired Munasan, and Reggae Cafe, as well as beach grills. Many premium-brand liquors are served at several bars throughout the property, which also has excellent spa, fitness, and tennis court facilities. There is also an underwater disco where "nuff tings a gwaan."

It's important to be aware of any special theme weeks being held at Hedo when booking, lest you should arrive and be expected to swap spouses with one of your fellow guests during Swingers' Week.

Sandals Negril (Long Bay, www.sandals. com, US$818–2,454 per night) is a 222-room resort on Negril's famed Seven-Mile Beach. The resort offers exclusive butler service in its top room category, a Red Lane Spa, two-story loft suites with spiral staircases, a pro sports complex offering racketball, squash and tennis, two pools, two whirlpool tubs, and a scuba certification pool. Swim-up river suites have stairs descending from the veranda doors into a lazy river with views out to sea, and plantation suites have private plunge pools, outdoor showers, and private balconies. Rooms have complete amenities, from cable TV to air-conditioning and en suite baths.

Sandals imposes a minimum stay of three nights at all its properties. Promotions are ongoing throughout the year, slashing rates by as much as 65 percent based on length of stay.

Club Hotel Riu Negril (tel. 876/957-5700, www.riu.com, US$228 and up) is a 420-room all-inclusive resort on Bloody Bay with a large main building and four two-story annexes. The resort has a gym, Jacuzzi, and sauna reserved for guests over 18. Rooms have mini-bars, king or two double beds, and a balcony or terrace. Four restaurants offer a la carte and buffet dining options, with bars spread across the property. The resort has two hard-surface tennis courts, table tennis, volleyball, and a variety of water sports. The hotel has a computer room available at an additional charge, with a free Wi-Fi zone for guests with laptops. The Renova Spa offers a variety of massages and treatments at an additional charge.

Riu Palace Tropical Bay (tel. 876/957-5900, www.riu.com) is a 416-room all-inclusive resort, also located on Bloody Bay, with

double rooms, junior suites, and suite categories. Renovated completely in 2008, rooms have mini-bars, cable TV, air-conditioning, lounge areas in junior suites, and en suite baths with verandas or balconies. The resort features several buffet and a la carte options, formal dress required in the fine dining restaurants for evening dinners. The hotel features 24-hour room service, a free Wi-Fi zone, and several bars and pool bars scattered throughout the property.

West End
UNDER US$100

Tip Top (turn inland on Red Ground Rd. at Scotia Bank, cell tel. 876/360-4857 or 876/435-7222) sits at the top of a hill in an area known as Red Ground. It's a popular spot for budget travelers from Europe, as well as for long-term stays. Rates start at US$25 for simple rooms with private bath and fan. For US$35 you get a kitchenette. Clean sheets and towels are provided. Marva Mathe manages the guesthouse, which has been in business for 30 years.

Khus Khus Negril (tel. 876/957-4263, reservations@khuskhusnegril.com, www.khuskhusnegril.com, US$87–117) is an affordable option that puts comfort first—with an appreciable departure from the floral bed covers so typical of run-of-the-mill hotels across Jamaica. Blue Mountain Aromatics toiletries, iPod docking stations, and complimentary Wi-Fi complement the soothing linens to make Khus Khus a pleasurable retreat. Khus Khus has a total of 27 rooms, with room categories like "satisfy my soul," which has two double beds, "one love a queen," with one standard bed, the premium "garden peace suites," and "cease and settle" suites with a queen bed and pull-out couch. All rooms have a mini-fridge and iPod docks, comfortable lighting, and a sleek atmosphere. Several units surround a small pool in the back courtyard, while a restaurant and bar are in a second courtyard closer to the office and parking area.

Xtabi (tel. 876/957-0121, fax 876/957-0827, xtabiresort@cwjamaica.com, www.xtabi-negril.

com) is one of the most accommodating properties in Negril in terms of the price range for the rooms on offer and value for your money. From economy rooms (US$49/65 low/high season) with fans to spacious suites (US$59/90 low/high season) with air-conditioning and TV to stylish cliff-top cottages (US$120/210 low/high season), there is something for every budget. The restaurant and bar, also on the cliffs, serve up some of the best lobster (US$25) in Negril, and the conch burger is highly acclaimed. Xtabi is the most unpretentious, well-situated hotel on the West End. The name Xtabi is Greek for "meeting place of the gods."

Prim-Rose Inn (tel. 876/771-0069 or 876/640-2029, US$20/35 low/high season) is a real shoestring joint run by Gasnel Hylton. It has five basic rooms featuring fans, hot water, and hammocks on a porch. The inn is set back on the bush side of West End Road. The driveway is marked by a sign for Haciender Inn; Prim-Rose is about 100 meters from the main road on the left.

US$100-250

Negril Escape and Spa (tel. 876/957-0392, info@negrilescape.com, www.negrilescape.com, US$90/180 low/high season) offers a variety of themed accommodations: the Oriental Express, Passage to India, Romancing the Kasba, Back to Africa, Atlantis, Negril Cottage, and Coconut Grove. Some of these are more tasteful than others, but the fact that a variety of options are offered is well appreciated by its returning guests, who found the recent renovations a welcome infusion of color. Rooms come with all the basic amenities including hot water, air-conditioning, cable TV, clean sheets and towels, and Internet in the main office. If diving is on your agenda, it's a great base.

Negril Escape has earned a well-deserved reputation as a nightlife hotspot on Negril's West End. On Tuesday nights the hotel hosts some of Jamaica's top billing reggae and dancehall artists in its beautiful oceanfront setting. Acts have included Queen Ifrica, Taurus Riley, Jah Cure, Shaggy, and Wayne Wonder, among many others.

Catch a Falling Star (tel. 876/957-0390, stay@catchajamaica.com, www.catchajamaica.com, US$95–175 low season, US$120–250 high season) has five one-bedroom cottages, two two-bedroom cottages, and a recently completed thatch-roofed building on the cliffs with six units. With its cliff-top grounds well maintained with neat walkways and verdant gardens, this is one of the choice properties on the West End.

◖ Banana Shout (tel. 876/957-0384, cell tel. 876/350-7272, reservations@bananashoutresort.com, www.bananashoutresort.com, US$80–100 low season, US$150–200 high season) is owned by Milo Gallico, named after the Mark Conklin novel of the same name about Jamaica. It's a beautifully decorated property on one of the West End's most gorgeous stretches of cliffs. Four one- and two-bedroom cottages adorn the cliffs with cozy furniture and an artsy vibe. A live band performs classic reggae covers every evening from Rick's Cafe next door, for an earful of music to set the mood for sunset.

Banana's Garden (across West End Road from Rick's Cafe, tel. 876/957-0909, cell tel. 876/353-0007, bananasgarden@gmail.com, www.bananasgarden.com, US$85–135 low season, US$100–165 high season), owned and operated by Nicole Larson, is a tasteful retreat with five quaint, self-contained cottages surrounded by lush vegetation. Each cottage has unique, hand-carved wood trim detailing, ceiling fans, louvered windows, hot water, and kitchenettes, making the property ideal for those looking for independence and the modest, back-to-basics vibe that put Negril on the map. The pool is beautiful. The property operates as a B&B, with rates including a continental or Jamaican breakfast. Banana's Garden is ideal for small groups looking to book the entire property, for which discounts can be negotiated. The Solar Wellness Spa on property offers massage and treatments.

OVER US$250

Rockhouse (tel. 876/957-4373, fax. 876/957-0557, info@rockhousehotel.com, www.rockhousehotel.com) is a favorite for hip New York

© OLIVER HILL

Widely regarded as the best boutique all-inclusive resort in Jamaica, The Caves pampers its guests in cliffside bliss.

weekenders looking to get away in style. The hotel is always booked, testament to good marketing, quality service, well-maintained grounds, and competent management. The beautiful villas (US$295–350 low, US$355–425 high season) are perched on the cliffs with views out to sea. A total of 34 rooms include standards (US$125/160 low/high season) and studios (US$150/185 low/high season). The restaurant has a nice evening ambience—and the coconut-battered shrimp are a must. The pool is also notable for its assimilation with the cliffs. An eight-room spa offering massages, wraps, scrubs and holistic treatments using all-natural local ingredients is a recent addition to the property and includes two cliff-side treatment cabanas.

Rockhouse took over Pirates Cave Restaurant located next door in early 2009, renaming it Pushcart Restaurant to promote a rootsy Jamaican vibe, referencing the traditional handcart commonplace at the country's open-air markets.

◖ **The Caves** (tel. 876/957-0270, fax 876/957-4930, thecaves@cwjamaica.com, www.islandoutpost.com) is Negril's most vibesy upscale hotel. Thatch-roofed, contoured cottages are seamlessly integrated with the cliffs. The property is perfectly conducive to spiritual relaxation, with its sophisticated African motif, soft music floating on the breeze, and hot tubs carved into the cliffs like they belong there. At the same time, you're never far from the greatest adrenaline rush of your life, thanks to the many cliff-tops from which to vault into the crystal-clear waters—as much as 18 meters below. Everywhere you turn there are platforms for sunbathing or for diving. At night, a large grotto just above water level is strewn with flowers and set up as the most romantic dining room imaginable, lit with hundreds of candles.

Bertram and the late Greer-Ann Saulter teamed up with former Island Records boss Chris Blackwell to create their idea of paradise at The Caves. The rooms are all unique with king-size beds, African batik pillow covers, classic louvered windows, and well-appointed baths. Cozy wooden ceilings and whitewashed walls create a soothing ambience, and love seats are nestled into the surroundings wherever they fit. The cottages are decorated with an assortment of Jamaican carvings and paintings. Every detail at The Caves is consciously designed to set guests in a relaxed mode—to the point of entrancement. Open bars (some manned, some self-serve) dot the property, and a snack bar has gourmet food ready whenever you're hungry.

Rooms range from one-bedroom suites (US$615/800 low/high season) to two-bedroom cottages (US$720/915 low/high season). Perhaps the nicest two-bedroom cottage, Moon Shadow, is separated from the rest by The Sands bar, which is open to the public for sunset and features a balcony overlooking the lighthouse and an azure cove below. All suites have king-size beds, while the two-bedroom cottages have queen-size beds downstairs.

Tensing Pen (tel. 876/957-0387, fax 876/957-0161, tensingpen@cwjamaica.com, www.tensingpen.com) is the West End's crown gem. Luxurious, thatch-roofed, bungalow-style cottages adorn the cliffs above lapping turquoise waters. The absence of TVs in the cottages is deliberate, as is every other meticulous detail that makes Tensing Pen so hard to leave. The staff at Tensing Pen exhibit the epitome of Jamaican warmth. They all conspire to make guests feel a deep sense of belonging. They treat guests with the utmost attentiveness and the highest regard for those minute details that create the most pleasant and relaxing environment on earth, from the hibiscus flowers on your pillow to cool water at the bedside. An infinity-edge 16-by 30-foot saltwater pool was recently installed in front of the dining area and is fed by a rock fountain.

Moon Dance Cliffs (www.moon-danceresorts.com, from US$225/275 low/high season) is a sleek, modern property completed in 2008, located on the West End about a mile past the lighthouse and offering a combination of rooms in the main building

and villas. The resort offers all-inclusive and European plan packages. Villas come with a personal butler who attends to every need, from morning to night. Moon Dance Cliffs villas lack nothing, with stereos, computers, and phones in the living area with plush couches and a bar, outdoor patios with breakfast tables and lounge chairs overlooking the sea, and private whirlpool tubs in the yard just outside the master bedrooms.

Jackie's on the Reef (tel. 876/957-4997 or 718/469-2785, jackiesonthereef@rcn.com, www.jackiesonthereef.com, US$125/150 d low/high season) is the place to go for a nature, yoga, or tai chi retreat. The rates include morning activity sessions and are a great value. The hotel is one of the farthest out along West End Road, where there's less development and it's easy to meditate undisturbed.

The Westender Inn (tel. 876/957-4991, from US toll-free 800/223-3786, cell tel. 876/473-8172, westenderinn@yahoo.com, www.westenderinn.com, US$90–199) is a low-key accommodation a bit farther out from Jackie's, deep on the West End. Rooms are comfortable with polyester bed covers on a variety of bed sizes, and layouts from studios to one-bedrooms to oceanside suites. The hotel has a raised pool and deck with a restaurant and bar by the main parking area where nonguests are welcome.

Windrush Negril Bed & Breakfast (Orange Hill, tel. 876/425-5621 or 876/412-0794, from the U.S. tel. 508/873-1158 or 508/667-1257, windrushnegril@gmail.com, www.windrushnegril.com, US$175–225/day or US$1,400/week d, add US$25 per person nightly for extras) accommodates up to six guests between the bamboo house, a private cottage with a king-size bed, and a twin cot in an adjacent room, and Blue Snapper, a room on the ground level of the main house with a separate entrance, also with a king-size bed and a twin. There are two pools on the property, one fed by the lapping waves carved out of the low, coral cliffs at the seaside, and a freshwater pool by the main house. A boccie ball court makes the place singular in Negril.

NEGRIL

Meals are prepared to order in an idyllic open-air kitchen (not included in room rate). Windrush prioritizes the private, exclusive experience. To get to Windrush, keep straight where the main turns left up to Good Hope.

COTTAGES AND VILLAS

❰ Llantrisant Beach House (tel. 876/957-4259, cell tel. 305/467-0331, U.S. tel. 305/668-9877, info@beachcliff.com www. beachcliff.com), owned by Dr. and Mrs. Travis, is a unique property in that it is extremely proximate to everything in Negril. Llantrisant sits out on a point just west of the roundabout with a perfect view over Long Bay and Seven-Mile Beach. Rates are reasonable, given the luxury of having a tennis court and two private beaches (ranging US$320/400 low/high season for two persons to US$530/660 low/high season for up to the maximum occupancy of 11). Three meals per day cost an extra US$30 per person. A friendly and committed staff include two housekeepers, a groundskeeper, and night watchmen.

Hide Awhile (three-minute drive west of the lighthouse, tel. 876/957-9079, www.jamaica-jane.com, www.idleawhile.com) is Negril's most exclusive and luxurious private villa complex. Best for those looking for independence away from the hustle and bustle, the three villas feature a duplex layout with a spacious master bedroom upstairs. Amenities include all the details expected in a top-end property, from flat-panel televisions to a fully equipped kitchen, plush bedding, and a porch that puts all worries to rest. The property is ideally suited for those with a car and provides guests with a remote control to open the gate, giving the feel of a 007 retreat. Wireless Internet is available. Chisty (cell tel. 876/841-5696) is the Rastafarian caretaker who serves up excellent cooking.

Tingalayas (tel. 876/957-0126, reservations@tingalayasretreat.com) is named after a donkey, Tingalaya, that lives on the property. It has two independent cottages plus five rooms in two bigger cottages with a big communal kitchen. Owned by David

Rosenstein, Tingalayas is a good place for a group or family, with accommodations for up to 14 people. Amenities include ceiling fans, hot water, wireless Internet, and a combination of queen-size and bunk beds. Breakfast is included and resident Rasta cook Jubey does excellent lobster, jerk chicken, and rice and peas to order.

FOOD
Seven-Mile Beach
JAMAICAN

Best in the West is Negril's favorite jerk chicken spot; it's located directly across the road from Idle Awhile.

Rainbow Arches (Joy James, tel. 876/957-4745) has excellent curry shrimp and curry goat to order. The James family is one of oldest Jamaican families in Negril.

❰ Niah's Patties (10 A.M.–8 P.M. daily Dec. 15–May 15) at Wavz Entertainment Centre, has been making the best patties in Negril, and perhaps all of Jamaica, since

© OLIVER HILL

Niah takes the prize for best patty in Negril, if not all of Jamaica.

2005. Patty fillings include Italian, fish, red bean, potato, chicken, vegetable, and lobster (US$3.50–7).

Spring Park Restaurant (across from Mariposa, cell tel. 876/373-8060 or 876/401-5162, 8 A.M.–10 P.M. daily, US$5–10), is run by Henry Gardener, a pig farmer who makes the best roast pork around, as well as fried and grilled chicken. Henry also does Jamaican breakfast every day.

Ossie's Jerk Centre (opposite The Palms, tel. 876868-5858, 10 A.M.–10 P.M. daily, US$5–10, cash only), serves the best steamed fish and jerk on the beach. A beer costs about US$2.

Sonia's (across from Roots Bamboo, 8 A.M.–9 P.M. daily, US$5–10) is well recognized for her delicious Jamaican cuisine and homemade patties.

◖ **Sweet Spice** (Whitehall Rd., tel. 876/957-4621, 8:30 A.M.–10:30 P.M. daily, US$5–25) is the best place along the main road heading toward Sav for typical Jamaican fare at local prices. Sweet Spice is the most popular restaurant with locals for good reason, offering refreshing real-world value in a town where prices are more regularly on par with U.S. cities. Dishes like fried chicken, coconut curry, or escoveitch fish, conch, and lobster are representative of Jamaica's traditional cuisine.

Peppa Pot (Whitehall Rd., tel. 876/957-3388, 9 A.M.–8 P.M. Mon.–Sat., US$4–10) is located a bit farther down Whitehall Road heading east out of Negril. It's a popular local joint for jerk, as well as steamed fish with the requisite sides of breadfruit and festival.

Ackee Tree Restaurant (Whitehall Road, across from the Texaco station, cell tel. 876/871-2524, 8 A.M.–10 P.M. daily, US$5–8) serves the best Ital stew and local dishes and is frequented by popular artists in the know. Noel "Wall" Masters runs the joint.

Tasty Delight (Fire Station Rd., no phone) is the favorite restaurant of local taxi drivers, with typical Jamaican dishes at local rates.

Beach Road SeaFood Restaurant (across from Roots Bamboo, cell tel. 876/371-9643, 8 A.M.–9 P.M. Mon.–Sat., free delivery) serves fish, lobster, soursop fish, conch, and shrimp.

Devon "Tiger" Reid is the shop owner. **Late Night Hot Spot Bar** is located next door.

Rankcle Stankcle fish shop, run by Owen Keith Oliver "Taurus" Morgan (cell tel. 876/401-2503), operates out of a riverside corner of the Negril Fishing Cooperative.

The Black Star Line is an Ital restaurant located at Bongo's Farm in Sheffield, serving natural foods out of calabash bowls, natural juices, and jelly coconut water. The eatery is open by reservation only.

FINE DINING AND INTERNATIONAL

Charela Inn (tel. 876/957-4277, 7:30 A.M.–9:30 P.M. daily) serves vegetarian, chicken, fish, steak, lobster, and shrimp dinner entrées (US$20–48) and has good Jamaican and international dishes with a large selection of wines.

◖ **Kuyaba** (tel. 876/957-4318, 7 A.M.–11 P.M. daily, US$12–27) has consistently decent, but pricey, international and Jamaican fusion cuisine, including pork kebab, brown stew conch, peppered steak, and seafood linguine lobster for main courses.

Whistling Bird Private Club for Fine Dining (at Whistling Bird villas, tel. 876/957-4403, 7 A.M.–7 P.M., by reservation only) specializes in gourmet five-course meals (US$35) that offer a choice of dishes that include "Grandma's Favourite" pepperpot soup, pineapple chicken, escovitch fish, stuffed grouper, and bourbon rock lobster.

The Lobster House (at Sunrise Club, beside Coral Seas Garden, tel. 876/957-4293, noon–11 P.M. daily) serves Italian and Jamaican food: Dishes range from pasta with tomato sauce (US$8) to gnocchi (US$12), pizza baked in a wood-fired brick oven (US$10–16), and grilled lobster (US$26). Wines are about US$24–26, and great coffee is served.

The Boat Bar (between Rondel Village and Mariposa, tel. 876/957-4746, 8 A.M.–10 P.M. daily, US$10–30) is a favorite that has been serving chicken, fish, shrimp, goat, pork, and steak since 1983. The garlic lobster gets rave reviews. Bunny and Angie are the proprietors. A webcam is set up on Fridays, viewable at www.realnegril.com, to allow fans to keep in touch.

Ristorante da Gino (at Mariposa Hideaway, tel. 876/957-4918, 7 A.M.–11 P.M. daily) is a good Italian restaurant managed by Vivian Reid, the wife of the late Gino. He was killed in 2005, allegedly by Italian thugs. The menu includes mixed salad (US$5), spaghetti alioli (US$10), linguine lobster (US$20), grilled lobster (US$25), and mixed grilled fish (US$30). A complete breakfast (US$10) comes with eggs and bacon, toast, fruit, juice, and coffee. Gino's also has a decent selection of Italian wines.

Marley's by the Sea does breakfast (8 A.M.–10 P.M.), lunch by the beach grill, and dinner with a rotating menu including items like shrimp linguini (US$15) or pan-fried pork and mozzarella (US$18).

Pancake House at Firefly (tel. 876/957-4358, 7 A.M.–10 P.M.) serves breakfast all day, with pancakes, eggs, French toast, and breakfast sandwiches. Cheapest Red Stripe on the beach (US$1.50) is here.

◖ Cosmos Seafood Restaurant and Bar (next door to Beaches Negril, tel. 876/957-4330, 9 A.M.–10 P.M. daily, US$5–43) serves excellent Jamaican seafood dishes, including conch soup, shrimp, and fried fish—in addition to other local dishes like curry goat, stewed pork, fried chicken, and oxtail. The beach out front is wide and good for swimming. A mix of Jamaican, expat, and tourist clientele, perhaps even weighted toward the local crowd, is testament to the reasonable prices and tasty Jamaican home-style cooking.

Chill Awhile (at Idle Awhile Resort, tel. 876/957-3303, 7 A.M.–9 P.M. daily) offers free lounge chairs and wireless Internet for its customers. The charming beachfront deck restaurant serves a variety of light food items for lunch including club sandwiches, burgers, fish and chips (US$6–8), and jerk chicken (US$10). For dinner, international and Jamaican-style entrées range from grilled chicken breast with peanut or Jamaican sauce (US$8.50) and coconut-breaded snapper with tartar sauce (US$12.50) to lobster thermidor (US$23.50) or a seafood platter with grilled lobster and

coconut shrimp (US$25). There is also a full bar next to the restaurant.

Norma's on the Beach (at Sea Splash Resort, tel. 876/957-4041, 7:30 A.M.–10 P.M. daily) is owned by the legendary Jamaican culinary dynamo Norma Shirley, who has contributed recipes and menus at numerous fine dining restaurants in Jamaica, starting with her flagship Norma's on the Terrace in Kingston. Her pioneering Jamaican and Caribbean fusion dishes attracted wide acclaim, even if it would seem on occasion that her reputation and pricing have outgrown the cuisine. A third restaurant under Norma's tutelage is based at the Errol Flynn Marina in Port Antonio.

West End

Hammond's Pastry Place (at the roundabout, tel. 876/957-4734, 8 A.M.–6 P.M. Mon.–Sat.) serves patties, cakes, and deli sandwiches.

Juicy J's (behind Scotiabank, tel. 876/957-4213, 7 A.M.–10 P.M. daily, US$4–15) is a popular local joint serving typical Jamaican dishes at low cost.

◖ Sea View Bar & Grill (West End Rd., around the bend from Scotia Bank, tel. 876/957-9191, 4 P.M.–2:30 A.M. daily), run by Tony Montana, does the best steam roast conch (US$2) around, as well as steam roast fish (US$4–11), conch soup (US$1/US$1.50) and jerk chicken (US$4).

Seaview House Chinese Restaurant (Cotton Tree Place, between Vendors' Plaza and the Post Office, tel. 876/957-4925, 10 A.M.–10 P.M. daily) has decent Chinese food. It serves vegetable dishes (US$7–10), chicken (US$10), seafood (US$18), and roast duck and lobster variations (US$27).

Mi Yard (located across from the Houseboat, tel. 876/957-4442, www.miyard.com) serves snack items like fish, egg, cheese, or ham and cheese sandwiches, as well as Jamaica's favorite starchy food snacks or accompaniments like plantain, festival, breadfruit, and bammy. Meals are done to order and include items like cabbage and carrot cooked down, curry chicken, brown stew chicken, and fish (US$3–4). Eight computers are available for Internet browsing by purchasing a card (US$3.50 per hour). It is a 24-hour restaurant and an especially convenient and popular spot for a late-night bite.

Canoe Beach Bar & Grill (across from MX3, tel. 876/957-4814, or Kirby's cell tel. 876/878-5893, canoebeachbar@gmail.com) serves Jamaican favorites at reasonable prices.

✦ Mary's Bay Restaurant & Boat Bar (tel. 876/957-0981 or 876/819-3005, 10 A.M.–10 P.M. daily, US$3–25) serves a variety of seafood like grouper, mahimahi, tuna, and snapper. It is also the home of "the serious burger," a double patty layered with mushrooms and bacon. Scottish couple Janet and Alan Young took over in May 2009, infusing the seaside setting with a relaxing ambiance true to the original laidback vibe that put Negril on the map. They serve a great mix of Jamaican favorites and international dishes at competitive prices.

✦ Blue Water Internet Cafe (One Love Drive, tel. 876/957-0125, or contact proprietor Randy cell tel. 876/884-6030, randysbluewater@yahoo.com, www.bluewaterinternetnegril.com, 8 A.M.–11 P.M. daily, US$2 per 20 minutes) serves Jamaica's best gelato, Calypso Gelato. The Internet café has the best equipment in Negril with CD burning, fax, webcam, and inexpensive VoIP telephony. Pizza is made from scratch daily (US$2 per slice, US$19 for a large pie) and is some of the best in Negril. Internet costs US$5 on his computer or for Wi-Fi.

Jus Natural Restaurant Seafood and Vegetarian (next to Xtabi, across from La Kaiser, tel. 876/957-0235, 8 A.M.–9 P.M. daily, closed on Sundays in low season, US$6–30) serves breakfast, lunch, and dinner with items like calalloo or ackee omelettes and fresh juices. Vegetarian dishes and seafood items are served for lunch and dinner. The phone line can get waterlogged but comes back when it dries out, so clients are advised to simply "set out an' reach," or show up assuming it's open during normal business hours.

3 Dives Jerk Centre (contact owner Lyndon Myrie, a.k.a. Lloydie, tel. 876957-0845

or 876/782-9990, noon–midnight daily) offers a quarter chicken with bread (US$3.50) or with rice and peas and vegetables (US$4.50), half chicken with rice and peas and veggies (US$8), steamed or curried shrimp (US$17), and grilled lobster (US$34). This is *the* place to get jerk on the West End. Located right on the cliffs, the open-air restaurant has a nice outdoor barbecue vibe. The 3 Dives hosts the Negril Jerk Festival every November.

Pushcart Restaurant and Rum Bar (tel. 876/957-4373, www.rockhousehotel.com/pushcart.php, 3–10 P.M. daily, US$9–16) serves entrées including peppered shrimp, homemade jerk sausage, curry goat, and oxtail. Opened in early 2009, Pushcart brings a Jamaican street food experience to one of the West End's most exclusive accommodations enclaves. The name is derived from the pushcarts used by Jamaican street vendors across the island in open-air markets, whether for selling produce or cooked food. The pushcart provides the inspiration for the menu, which is inspired by street food from Jamaica and throughout the Caribbean. A lively local mento band provides nightly live entertainment. Pushcart offers casual dining in a breathtaking cliff-side setting made famous as a location in the films *20,000 Leagues Under the Sea* and the Steve McQueen classic, *Papillon*.

Ras Rody (across from Tensing Pen, 10 A.M.–6 P.M.) is an Ital food shop that specializes in soups, normally red pea soup (US$8–10) and other vegetarian specialties of the day.

The Health Shop (Tait's Plaza, tel. 876/957-4274, cell tel. 876/427-1253, 10 A.M.–6 P.M. Mon.–Thurs., 10 A.M.–4:30 P.M. Fri.) sells whole-wheat vegetarian patties, hearty juice blends, and other natural foods at local prices.

✦ The Hungry Lion (West End, tel. 876/957-4486, 4–10:30 P.M. daily, closed in Oct., US$8–24), under the ownership of Bertram Saulter, who also owns The Caves, is an excellent dinner spot with healthy-sized entrées. The lobster burritos are delicious. A pleasant atmosphere is created with irie music, carved faces, and mellow tones covering the walls. The Hungry Lion is good value for the money, and the drink special—the Lion Heart, made with mango, ginger, and rum—shouldn't be missed.

Royal Kitchen (Chef Errold Chambers, cell tel. 876/287-0549, 8 A.M.–11 P.M. daily, US$3–5) is one of the best spots in Negril for Ital vegetarian food, prepared Rasta style with excellent fresh juices to accompany the meal.

Erica's Cafe (cell tel. 876/889-3109, 5–10 P.M. daily) has excellent Jamaican staples. Many locals consider Erica's the best stewed chicken (US$5) on the island.

Sips & Bites (adjacent to Rock House, tel. 876/957-0188, 7 A.M.–10:30 P.M. Sun.–Thurs., 7 A.M.–5:30 P.M. Fri., closed Sat., US$5–10) is a good spot for breakfast and has good Jamaican dishes like fried chicken, curry goat, and oxtail.

Choices (across from Samsara, tel. 876/957-4841, 7 A.M.–11 P.M., US$4–7) is an earthy restaurant on the West End serving Jamaican fare like ackee and saltfish and steamed calalloo for breakfast, plus curry goat and fried chicken at moderate prices.

LTU Pub & Restaurant (tel. 876/957-0382, 7 A.M.–11 P.M. daily, US$10–30) has good Jamaican and international food in a laid-back setting perched on the cliffs. Specialties include crab quesadilla, stuffed jalapeño, and crab ball appetizers, plus schnitzel, surf and turf, pasta, chicken, and seafood dishes like grilled salmon and the snapper papaya boat. The name of the place is taken from the Germany-based airline Lufthansa Transport United, of which founder Walter Bigge was a shareholder. Bigge was killed in 1992 and the restaurant closed for a spell before being taken over by the present owner, Bill Williams, who bought the place around 2000. Wi-Fi is available free for customers.

Rick's Cafe (tel. 876/957-0380, noon–10 P.M. daily, US$18–28) is a moneymaker that has other business owners in Negril envious. It's worth stopping by for a look at the immense

© OLIVER HILL

Boutique resort Banana Shout, left, neighbors Rick's Cafe, the most popular sunset venue in Negril, where cliff jumping is the favored activity.

crowd that is bussed in each evening, making it one of Negril's most successful commercial ventures. The property was renovated in the recent past after a large chunk of cliff fell into the sea during a hurricane. A huge boom was erected for a rope swing, and there are plenty of platforms to jump off for all levels of adrenaline junkies. A diver in a Speedo climbs to the top of a tree for the highest dive of all, waiting for enough tips to be collected by his cohort before tucking into a cannonball for the 25-meter drop. Meanwhile, a live band belts out reggae classics throughout the evening, some of them coming across more true to the originals than others. Food and beer at Rick's is mediocre and outrageously expensive, but nobody seems to mind. Choices include chicken, shrimp, fish, and lobster with rice and peas, french fries, or sweet potato sides; a beer costs US$5. If you don't want to pay the cover (US$5) to get in at Rick's but still want to partake in the action, you can enjoy the same scene with a more local perspective from the outcropping next door behind an artist's shack, Jah Creation, where kids beg US$2 from the tourists to jump off the cliffs. There are plenty of better, more tranquil, and less hyped spots for cliff-jumping, including Pushcart Restaurant and The Sands, both of which are recommended.

The Sands is the best place to experience the West End's cliffs away from the gawking crowds that convene at Rick's each evening. It is a great bar, right next to the nicest and most secluded villa at Negril's top resort, and therefore a great way to experience The Caves' vibe if you can't stay there. There is a challenging-enough spot to jump into the water approximately 12 meters below—with the best view of Negril's lighthouse right next door. Professional jumpers come show off on Wednesday and Saturday, when jerk is served.

INFORMATION AND SERVICES

Negril has a very active online community (www.negril.com) where message boards, news, and events are posted, as well as advertising for hotels in Negril and beyond. Other relevant organizations include the Negril Resort Association (www.negriljamaica.com), which has special offers at select hotels.

Banking can be done at **NCB** (at Sunshine Village, tel. 876/957-4117; ATMs at Plaza Negril and Petcom) or **Scotiabank** (Negril Square, across from Burger King near the roundabout, tel. 876/957-4236; ATM at the Petcom next to the airstrip across from Breezes).

FX Trader (888/398-7233) has a branch at Hi-Lo supermarket in Sunshine Village Plaza by the roundabout (9 A.M.–5 P.M. Mon.–Thurs., 9 A.M.–5:30 P.M. Fri.–Sat.).

The Negril **police station** (tel. 876/957-4268, emergency dial 119) is located just beyond the roundabout on Nompriel Road. Negril police officer Dwayne advises travelers to stay away from dark, secluded areas at night, as people have had bags grabbed. Don't leave valuables on the beach while swimming, and take care not to get robbed by prostitutes. Prostitution is illegal but common and not prosecuted, the penalty being nominal in court.

The Negril **post office** (tel. 876/957-9654, 8 A.M.–5 P.M. Mon.–Fri.) is located on West End Road between Cotton Tree Hotel and Samuel's Hardware just past Vendor's Plaza.

The **Negril Chamber of Commerce** (Vendors Plaza, West End Rd., tel. 876/957-4067, www.negrilchamberofcommerce.com) has tourist information, including a regularly updated brochure full of ads for hotels and attractions.

Long Bay Medical & Wellness Centre (Norman Manley Blvd., tel. 876/957-9028) is run by Dr. David Stair.

Omega Medical Centre (White Swan Plaza and Sunshine Plaza, tel. 876/957-9307 or 876/957-4697) has two branches run by husband-and-wife team Dr. King and Dr. Foster.

Dr. Grant (Sunshine Plaza, West End, tel. 876/957-3770) runs a private clinic.

Negril Nightscape Tours (cell tel. 876/407-8414 or 876/407-8489, info@negrilnightscapetours.com, www.negrilnightscapetours.com) is a nightlife tour-company run by two young expats, Angela Eastwick and Danielle Velez, which offers an all-inclusive service that includes a driver, admission to the hotspot of the night, and drink specials.

Roge Croll (cell tel. 876/468-5001, rogecroll@yahoo.com) and his team offer photography and videography services for weddings or any other event you want to remember.

Internet Access

Complimentary Wi-Fi is found at most of the more modern hotels and restaurants in Negril, from Chill Awhile and Kristyl's Restaurant on the Beach to Canoe Bar & Grill and LTU Pub & Restaurant on the West End. For those traveling without a laptop, try **Sue's Easy Rock Internet Cafe** (tel. 876/957-0816 or cell tel. 876/424-5481, www.easyrockinternetcafe.com, US$2 for 30 minutes) which offers phone calls, fax, and breakfast all day at Mary's Bay, or **Lynks Internet Café & Gift Shop** (US$2 for 20 minutes), located beside Sips and Bites. Mi Yard (tel. 876/957-4442, www.miyard.com) offers Internet access for US$3.50/hour.

Blue Water Internet Café (One Love Drive, tel. 876/957-0125, or contact proprietor Randy, cell tel. 876/884-6030, randysbluewater@yahoo.com, www.bluewaterinternetnegril.com, 8 A.M.–11 P.M. daily) offers access on several desktops for US$2 per 20-minute interval, or US$5 per hour, with the best equipment in town for CD burning, fax, webcam, and inexpensive VoIP telephony. Wi-Fi is also available at the same rates if you bring your laptop.

GETTING THERE
Air

Negril's Aerodrome can accommodate small private aircraft and charters. The only operator in Jamaica currently offering charter flights to Negril is Jamaica Air Shuttle, which will take passengers in from Kingston and Montego Bay. Contact marketing manager Derrick Dwyer (tel. 876/923-0371, 876/923-0372, 876/923-0373, or 876/901-5196, ddwyer@jamaicaairshuttle.com) to schedule service. Charter fares run US$2,000 per hour, with any single flight around the island not lasting more than an hour, and as little as 15 minutes, depending on point of origin and destination.

Ground

Negril can be reached by several means, depending on your budget and comfort requirements. Most accommodations offer airport transfers at additional cost, and a host of private taxi operators generally charge around US$60 per couple, with an additional US$20 for extra passengers.

The best option for budget-minded travelers is booking an airport pickup or drop-off through the Jamaica Union of Travelers Association (JUTA) in cars, vans, and coaches of up to 45-person capacity. JUTA's Negril Chapter (Norman Manley Blvd., tel. 876/957-4620 or 876/957-9197, info@jutatoursnegrilltd.com, www.jutatoursnegrilltd.com) offers transfers for US$20 per person from the beach and US$25 from the cliffs, by far the most affordable way to get between Negril and Montego Bay's Sangster International Airport. Reservations made by email receive a US$2 discount. JUTA also takes tourists on excursions to popular attractions across the island.

For more personalized taxi and tour services, try **Alfred's Taxi and Tour Company** (tel. 876/854-8016 or 876/527-0050, or from U.S. tel. 646/289 4285, alfredstaxi@aol.com and negriltracy@aol.com, US$50 for two). Proprietor Alfred Barrett recently acquired a 15-seat bus, upping capacity and expanding on "Irie Airport Rides and Vibes" in his standard tinted Toyota Corolla station wagon.

For those with less money and more time, there are buses from Mobay to Savanna-la-Mar (US$2) and then from Sav to Negril (US$2), mainly serviced by route taxis. It is also possible to take a route taxi from Mobay to Hopewell (US$2), then another from Hopewell to Lucea (US$2), and then a third from Lucea to Negril US$2), but these cars leave when full and won't have much room for luggage.

Negril has two main taxi stands: one next to Scotiabank in Negril Square, where taxis depart for points along the West End following the cliffs; the other in the main park next to the police station on Whitehall Road, where taxis and buses depart for points along Norman Manley Boulevard and east toward Sav-la-Mar.

GETTING AROUND

Route taxis run up and down the coast from the Beach to the West End, generally using the plaza across from Burger King by the roundabout as a connection point. Some negotiating will generally be required, as the route taxis always try to get a higher fare from tourists, especially at night when everyone is charged extra. From anywhere on the West End to the roundabout should never be more than US$1.50 during the day, and as much as double at night. From there to the beach should also not cost more than US$1.50. Excursions beyond the beach and the West End can be arranged with private taxi and tour operators.

Hanover

Hanover is Jamaica's third-smallest parish after Kingston and St. Andrew, with roughly 451 square kilometers of land. It has six major rivers, two of which flow into Lucea Harbour. The Great River, along the border with St. James, has Jamaica's most heart-thumping navigable rapids in the hills of the interior, as well as serene bamboo rafting where it lazily meets the sea.

Lucea, Hanover's capital, sits on an idyllic horseshoe-shaped harbor a few kilometers from **Dolphin Head Mountain.** Dolphin Head is a small limestone peak at 545 meters, which overlooks some of the most biologically diverse forestland in Jamaica, with the island's highest concentration of endemic species. A few kilometers away, **Birch Hill**—at 552 meters—is the highest point in the parish. Together the small

© OLIVER HILL

Lucea's famous clock tower

range protects Lucea harbor from the dominant easterly winds. Both Lucea and Mosquito Cove are well-regarded hurricane holes for small yachts. Hanover is the only parish without a KFC.

HISTORY

Hanover exists as a parish since it was portioned off from Westmoreland in 1723 and given the name of English monarch George I of the House of Hanover. The Spanish first settled the area when New Seville was abandoned in 1534 and the capital moved to Spanish Town. Lucea became prosperous, with a busier port than Montego Bay in its heyday, which served 16 large sugar estates in the area. Remnants of many estate great houses dot the landscape to the east and west of Lucea, their abandoned ruins showing evidence of having been torched and destroyed during slave riots. Kennilworth, Barbican, and Tryall are a few of the old estates that have visible ruins; although they have been declared national heritage sites, they are not maintained.

HOPEWELL TO TRYALL

Just west of Montego Bay, the Great River marks the border of St. James and Hanover, which represents Jamaica's high-end tourism. Before arriving at Round Hill, one of Jamaica's most exclusive club hotels, Tamarind Hill and its surrounding coastline are strewn with luxurious villas, most of which fetch upwards of US$10,000 per week during the high season.

The town of Hopewell is not especially remarkable beyond its present status as a somewhat active fishing community. There's a Scotiabank ATM, a small grocery store, and a few hole-in-the-wall restaurants for typical Jamaican fare in the heart of town. There is generally a sound system slowing traffic through town on Friday evenings, which precedes a busy market day on Saturday; if you're staying in the vicinity, it's worth a stop.

A few kilometers farther west of Round Hill and Hopewell is Tryall, a former sugarcane plantation destroyed during the Christmas Rebellion of 1831–1832. The old water wheel,

fed by an aqueduct from the Flint River, can be seen as you round the bend approaching Tryall from the east, but little else remains as a reminder of its past as a sugar estate. Today the hotel and villa complex, which fans out from the historic great house, sits on one of the Caribbean's premier golf courses; its winter residents include boxing champion Lennox Lewis.

Bordering Tryall to the west is a burgeoning bedroom community, Sandy Bay, where new housing developments are rapidly springing up. Still farther west, the highway wraps around Mosquito Cove, where sailboats create a flotilla to party the night away before Easter weekend in preparation for a morning race back to Mobay every year.

Accommodations

◖ **Round Hill Hotel and Villas** (tel. 876/956-7050, fax 876/956-7505, reservations@roundhilljamaica.com, www.roundhilljamaica.com, suites US$419–843 nightly low season, US$631–1,261 high season), just over the Great River, is an exclusive hotel and club on meticulously manicured grounds. The hotel's main Pineapple Suites, featuring plush lounge furniture, were designed by Ralph Lauren and boast an atmosphere of stately, oceanfront elegance. A host of returning guest luminaries has sealed Round Hill's well-deserved reputation for excellence.

In the Pineapple Suites, a series of hinged louvered windows open to overlook an infinity pool and the sea beyond, perfectly aligned for dreamy sunsets. The bathrooms feature rainwater showerheads above glass enclosures and large bathtubs. Just above the hotel suites, villas are strewn across the hillside, each surrounded by a maze of shrubs and flowers, ensuring the utmost privacy. Next to the small, calm beach there's a charming library with a huge TV (to make up for their absence in the suites) and an open-air dining area; a short walk down the coast leads to the spa, based in a renovated plantation great house. Villas at Round Hill (US$875–2,875 nightly low season, US$1,250–4,100 high) can be booked

COURTESY OF ROUND HILL/DAVID MASSEY

Round Hill Hotel and Villas is Jamaica's premiere waterfront resort.

through the hotel office. Round Hill rents a total of 27 villas.

Tryall Club (tel. 876/956-5660, U.S. tel. 800/238-5290, reservation@tryallclub.com, www.tryallclub.com, one-bedroom suites from US$395/550 low/high season) has private suites adjoining the main house, as well as villas scattered throughout the property that are pooled and rented through the club reservation office.

Tryall Villas rent for US$630–785 low season, US$1,185/1,570 high, for superior or deluxe category, respectively. They come fully staffed with excellent cooks who prepare delectable Jamaican favorites and are adept at international cuisine. Most suites and villas have a one-week minimum stay during the high season, reduced to three or four days during the low season. Given the villas are privately owned, certain owners establish their own low and high season dates and discounts, so these can vary.

Tryall has one of the top golf courses in the Caribbean; it sits on an 890-hectare estate that extends deep into the Hanover interior. Tennis and golf are offered to nonmembers (greens

fees are US$125 daily plus tax, carts are US$30 plus tax, and a caddy is US$30, plus a customary US$20 tip). Tryall guests pay substantially less (greens fees US$70/100 plus tax low/high season). There are nine tennis courts, two with lights. The cushioned courts are less slippery than the faux clay. Courts are for members and guests only and included in the stay. Related fees include US$23/hour for hitting partner, US$48 to play with a club pro, and US$7 per hour for a ball boy. At night, courts cost US$20 per hour for the lights.

The food at Tryall is an excellent value, while far from inexpensive, with Master Chef Herbert Baur demonstrating his wealth of experience in overseeing day-to-day operations. Meals are kept interesting with the Jamaican barbecue dinner on Wednesday, seafood buffet dinner on the beach on Friday, and open-air à la carte dining on the veranda of the main house on other evenings (7–9:30 P.M.). Tryall sources 95 percent of the produce it serves locally, as well as 100 percent of the chicken and pork.

Food

◖ **Charis Restaurant** (just before the entrance to Round Hill heading west, tel. 876/956-7530, or cell. 876/441-9992, Mon-Sat 9 A.M.–6 P.M., US$5–10) serves jerk chicken and pork, curry chicken and goat, a variety of pasta dishes including alfredo sauce, shrimp and chicken, or Rasta pasta with ackee, in season. Steamed, grilled, or fried fish is done to order. The restaurant reopened in January 2009 under the new ownership of two local couples, Geoffrey and Jackry Harris, and Marcine and Oniel Brown.

Sea Shells (cell tel. 876/436-9175, 9 A.M.–9 P.M. daily, US$7–21), just west of Hopewell, is run by Lorna Williams and serves chicken, pork, fish, and lobster dishes. The restaurant has a rootsy vibe, with the dining area right next to the water and a bar by the roadside.

◖ **Dervy's Lobster Trap** (cell tel. 876/783-5046, open by reservation daily, US$18–30), owned by the charismatic Dervent Wright, and operated by the whole family, including his wife Gem, daughter Tiffany, and son, Junior. Dervy's has some of the island's best lobster, plus a great view of Round Hill from its vantage point on the waterfront. Be sure to call ahead to make reservations. Reach it by taking the second right in Hopewell, heading west down Sawyer's Road to the sea's edge. A sign for Lobster Trap indicates the turnoff from the main road.

LUCEA TO GREEN ISLAND

Hanover's capital, Lucea is a quiet town that occasionally comes alive for special events like Independence Day, when the town hosts a talent show. Lucea's **Fort Charlotte,** which sits at the mouth of the harbor, was never used. The town was busier than Montego Bay at the height of the colonial period following emancipation and would become important for the export of molasses, bananas, and yams. The large Lucea yam, exported to Jamaican laborers in Cuba and Panama during the construction of railroads and the canal, is still an important product from the area today. The clock tower atop the historic 19th-century courthouse was originally destined for St. Lucia, but the town's residents liked it so much they refused to give it up in favor of the less ornate version they had commissioned by the same manufacturer in Great Britain.

Sights

Fort Charlotte, located on the point of Lucea Harbor, is the most intact fort in western Jamaica, with three cannons in good condition sitting on the battlements. It was built by the British in 1756, with 23 cannon openings to defend their colony from any challenge from the sea. Originally named Fort Lucea, it was renamed during the reign of King George III after his Queen Charlotte. The **Barracks,** a large rectangular Georgian building next to the fort, was built in 1843 to house soldiers stationed at Fort Charlotte. It was given to the people of Jamaica in 1862 by the English War Office; it became the town's education center and is now part of the high school complex.

Hanover Historical Museum (US$1.50 adults, US$0.50 children) is housed in the old police barracks and *gaol* (jail). It opened in 1989 and was at one point expanded to include artifacts from excavated Arawak middens (refuse piles) found in Hanover. The community museum has displays covering the history of Hanover from the Tainos to the present.

Kenilworth is one of Jamaica's most impressive great houses, located on the former Maggoty Estate. Currently the property is home to the HEART Academy, a training skills institute. To get there, pass Tryall and then Sandy Bay, then Chukka Blue; turn right after crossing a bridge over the Maggoty River in the community of Barbican and look for the sign for HEART Trust NTA Kenilworth on the left. Turn in and look for the ruins behind the institute, which is painted blue and white.

◖ Dolphin Head Mountain

Dolphin Head Mountain and the Dolphin Head Forest Reserve contain some of Jamaica's few remaining pockets of biodiversity and high endemism. A **Nature Trail** and **Living Botanical Museum** were developed over the past several years and are currently maintained by Jamaica's Forestry Department (contact regional manager Ian Wallace, iwallace@forestry. gov.jm, abromfield@forestry.gov.jm).

To reach the Dolphin Head Nature Trail and Live Botanical Museum, take the B9 inland from Lucea toward Glasgow. The trail starts in Riverside on the east side of the road a few kilometers before reaching Glagow. The trail was opened in February 2007 and leads along Retirement and Rugland mountains on the western flank of the Dolphin Head range. A second trail starts from Kingsvale leading into the forest reserve.

Accommodations and Food

The **Fiesta Group,** a Spain-based hotel chain, opened the 2,000-room Fiesta Paladium Palace (tel. 876/620-0000, www.fiestahotelgroup. com), a massive all-inclusive hotel just west of Lucea on Molasses beach in 2008.

Tapa Top Food Hut is located on the south side of the main road just east of the town center, with **Vital Ital** (contact Ray "Bongo Ray" Gonsalves, tel. 876/956-2218 or cell tel. 876/379-3423, 10 A.M.–10 P.M., Mon.–Sat.), on the harbor side of the road a few meters farther east. They serve a strictly vegan ital menu with dishes like tofu, stew, brown rice, veggie soup, and natural juices (US$2–5). Likewise, you can always count on a patty from **Juici Beef** (Mid Town Mall, tel. 876/956-3657) in the heart of Lucea on the west-bound circuit.

Services

NCB bank has a branch (tel. 876/956-2204) as well as an ATM location at Haughton Court.

Scotiabank (tel. 876/956-2235) has a branch on Willie Delisser Boulevard facing the main intersection by the courthouse on the western side of town.

Lailian Wholesale Supermarket is at Shop #14, Mid Town Mall (tel. 876/956-9712).

Family Care Pharmacy is at Shop #1, Mid Town Mall (tel. 876/956-2685).

Shoppers' Choice Supermarket is located in Green Island (tel. 876/955-2369).

BLENHEIM

Just before the one-way circuit around Lucea reaches the courthouse heading west, the B9 leads inland through Middlesex to Dias, where a right-hand turn leads back toward the coast and Davis Cove. About five kilometers west of Dias is Blenheim, the birthplace of Jamaica Labour Party founder William Alexander Clarke, who later took the name Bustamante after traveling and living in several Latin American countries. Blenheim is a quiet village with a simple museum devoted to the national hero popularly known as "Busta." The museum is located inside a re-created house, built by the National Heritage Trust after Busta's original house was destroyed by fire. More of a thatch-roofed hut, the house's interior has newspaper clippings and pictures of Sir Alexander adorning the walls.

GREEN ISLAND TO NEGRIL
Mandela Green Entertainment Centre

Established over a decade ago, Mandela Green is an entertainment lawn inside a walled compound, its interior walls painted with portraits of Jamaican artists and heroes in typical Rasta

style. It's used for parties, stage shows, theatrical performances, and other private and public functions. The entertainment center was revitalized over the past couple of years, opening a restaurant and bar (11 A.M.–11 P.M. daily) serving Jamaican dishes and seafood (US$5–10) in mid-2009. Contact Paul Taylor (cell tel. 876/871-8454, grentertainment1@gmail.com) for info and bookings.

According to Palma Taylor, Paul's father, who controls the property, the venue has given several up-and-coming Jamaican singers a *buss,* or career break, over the years.

◖ Half Moon Beach

Orange Bay, just west of Green Island, is a quiet little community with the idyllic **Half Moon Beach,** managed by Tania and Andrew Bauwen (cell tel. 876/827-1558 or 876/531-4508, halfmoonbeach1@hotmail.com, www.abingdonestate.com) just east of Rhodes Hall Plantation. Half Moon is a great place to come for a more low-key alternative to Negril's often-crowded Seven-Mile Beach.

Half Moon Beach Bar & Grill (7 A.M.–10 P.M. or until the last person leaves the bar) serves breakfast, lunch, and dinner in a laid-back beach shack setting, with typical Jamaican favorites as well as creative international fusion like shrimp with pineapple, sweet pepper kabob, seafood crepes, and lobster on the menu (US$5–18).

Accommodation is offered at Half Moon Beach in a number of cabins (cash only). Coconut Cabin (US$65) is a one-bedroom with a bathroom, ceiling fan, and mini fridge. Blue Moon Cabin (US$75) has two bedrooms that share a bathroom, sleeping up to four, plus ceiling fans and mini fridge. Seagrape I (US$65) and Seagrape II (US$65) each have one bed and bath with ceiling fans; they share a balcony. Half Moon Beach is one of the few places in Jamaica ideal for camping for those with their own tent (US$15).

Half Moon Beach is a great location for weddings, and the reefs offshore make for great snorkeling.

Rhodes Hall Plantation (tel. 876/957-6883

or 876/957-6422, rhodesresort@comcast.net, www.rhodesresort.com, US$95–340) sits on a 223-hectare estate adjacent to Orange Bay. Far enough removed from the hustle and bustle of Negril to feel neither the bass thumping at night nor the harassment during the day, Rhodes Hall has enough outdoor activities to not feel like you're missing anything either. The most recent addition to the list is the Rhino Safari on inflatable speedboats that will take you to cruise Seven-Mile Beach in no time. Other activities include horseback riding, hiking, and birding. A variety of modern, comfortable rooms, suites, and villas all have verandas with views out to sea. Satellite TV, air-conditioning, cell phones, queen-size beds, and hot water are standard. Ignore the floral bedcovers and focus on the woodwork and bamboo detailing, much of which was handcrafted from materials sourced on the property. Rates vary depending on size and amenities, which include three bathrooms, full kitchen, dining room, and whirlpool tub in the largest villa.

Savanna-la-Mar and Vicinity

Along the route from Negril to Savanna-la-Mar, the hills open up a few kilometers east from the beach to vast alluvial plains along Cabarita River that sustain Jamaica's largest sugarcane crop, processed at Frome. Small communities like Negril Spot and Little London dot the route and offer little excuse to stop. A turn off the main road in Little London leads to Little Bay, one of Jamaica's most laid-back beach towns, which is predominantly the keep of small-scale fishermen.

LITTLE BAY AND HOMER'S COVE

About 1.5 kilometers farther east from Homer's Cove is Little Bay, another rootsy fishing village relatively untouched by the outside world. Little Bay was a cherished retreat for Bob Marley, who would come to escape the pressures of Kingston and his burgeoning career.

Accommodations

Purple Rain Guest House (call Cug, pronounced "Cudge," cell tel. 876/425-5386, or book through Donna Gill Colestock at U.S. tel. 508/816-6923, greenbiscuit03@hotmail.com) is a small cottage set back from the beach owned by Livingston "Cug" Drummond. It's a basic cottage with two rooms in the downstairs and a loft with ceiling fans and lukewarm water. Rates are US$60 per person or US$400 per week, which includes two meals a day.

[Tansobak Seaside Cottage (U.S. tel. 608/873-9391 or 608/873-8195, mmoushey55@aol.com, www.littlebaycottages.com) is a tastefully appointed accommodation a few meters from the water's edge in Little Bay. It has simple but comfortable decor, louvered windows, tiled floors, and hot water. Air-conditioning is available by request. Denis and Michelle Dale have owned the property since the mid-1990s. Rates run US$665 per person per week, which includes two meals a day. There is a minimum three-night stay for double occupancy.

Coral Cove Resort & Spa (2 Old Hope Road, U.S. tel. 217/649-0619, cell tel. 876/457-7594, cclbayj@yahoo.com, www.coralcovejamaica.com, US$250–330 d all-inclusive) is a lovely five-acre property with a quarter mile of ocean frontage and 16 well-appointed rooms that have en suite bathrooms and wooden furniture. Beds are mostly king-size with a few queen and twin setups available. The property does a lot of wedding business and places an emphasis on fine cuisine. The family members who run the hotel go back and forth between Jamaica and their home in Illinois. Steven Zindars bought the land and started building in 1997 and opened the rental business in 1999, later buying an adjacent piece of land to expand toward Homer's Cove in 2004.

Food

Tiki's Guinep Tree Restaurant & Bar (in front of Uncle Sam's, tel. 876/438-3496, 10 A.M.–9 P.M., US$3.50–5), run by Vernon "Tiki" Johnson, is a favorite with locals. It serves dishes like stewed conch, fried fish, fried chicken, and jerk pork, accompanied with rice and peas or french fries.

Uncle Sam's Garden Park (next to sea, tel. 876/867-2897, US$1–3), run by Tiki's uncle, Samuel "Uncle Sam" Clayton, serves fried chicken, fried fish, and conch soup.

BROUGHTON BEACH

Broughton Beach is a secluded eight-kilometer-long beach reached by taking a right at the gas station in Little London, followed by a left at the T junction. Keep left at the Y junction and you will come to the parking lot of the Lost Beach Hotel on Brighton Beach. It is principally a fishing beach, but it has nice, fine white sand and an open expanse free of peddlers and hustlers.

Blue Hole Mineral Spring (Brighton, cell tel. 876/860-8805, www.blueholeinjamaica.com, 9 A.M.– 11 P.M. Mon.–Thurs., 9 A.M.–2 A.M. Fri.–Sun.) is a sink hole mineral spring located along the coast in Brighton suitable for jumping and swimming. A manmade swimming pool is fed with mineral water from the spring, and a bar keeps visitors cool, even if they're not inclined to jump into either pools.

SAVANNA-LA-MAR

Savanna-la-Mar, or simply Sav, as it is commonly referred to by locals, is one of the most subdued parish capitals in Jamaica in terms of attractions, with a few notable exceptions—namely the annual Curry Festival held in July behind Manning's School, and Western Consciousness, held in April at Paradise Park on the eastern outskirts of town. A free concert and symposium are also held in Sav every year in October to commemorate the life of the late Peter Tosh, who was born a few kilometers away in Grange Hill.

Sights

Manning's School, the most architecturally appealing building in town, is one of Jamaica's oldest schools, established in 1738 after local proprietor Thomas Manning left 13 slaves with land and what it could offer as the endowment for a free school. Now serving as a high school, the attractive wooden structure (built in late-colonial style in 1910 on the site of the original school) is backed by newer, less stylish concrete buildings set around a large field.

◖ Roaring River and Blue Hole Garden

Ten minutes from Savanna-la-Mar off of the B8, Roaring River and Blue Hole Garden (tel. 876/446-1997, 8 A.M.–5 P.M. daily) make for a good day trip from Negril or Bluefields. The Roaring River cave guided tour costs US$5 per person. Expect to be aggressively approached as soon as you near the main building for the site. Tipping the guide is also expected.

If you are headed for the Blue Hole, the real highlight of the park, continue farther up the road to the Lover's Cafe and guest cottages provide access to Blue Hole Garden (US$7). The Blue Hole is one of Jamaica's most spectacular subterranean springs, welling up in a refreshing turquoise pool.

◖ Mayfield Falls

The Original Mayfield Falls (tel. 876/610-8612 or cell tel. 876/457-0759, info@mayfieldfalls.com, www.mayfieldfalls.com) operates a four- to five-hour tour costing US$85 per person, inclusive of roundtrip transportation from Mobay, entry fee with a guided hike up the river, and lunch afterward. The entry fee is significantly lower (US$15) for those with their own transportation, inclusive of guide. Lunch may be purchased separately (US$10–22). Located in Flower

© OLIVER HILL

The current at Mayfield Falls can send you scampering for the banks.

Hill near the Hanover border, Mayfield Falls is one of the best waterfall attractions in Jamaica, having been developed with minimal impact to the natural surroundings. It's a great place to spend an afternoon cooling off in the river and walking upstream along a series of gentle cascades and pools. Run by Sarah Willis, the guided tour begins and ends at a group of buildings that house a gift shop and restaurant. Rubber Crocs shoes are rented for US$6 for those without their own waterproof footwear.

Mayfield Falls can be reached from either the North or South Coasts. From the North Coast, turn inland before crossing the bridge at Flint River on the eastern side of Tryall Estate and follow Original Mayfield signs. From the South Coast, turn inland in Sav, keeping straight ahead at the stoplight by the gas station on the east side of town rather than turning right toward Ferris Cross, and head straight toward the communities of Strathbougie, then take a left off Petersfield main road toward Hertford at the four-way

intersection. From Hertford, head toward Williamsfield and then to Grange, before making a right in the square to continue on for about 10 minutes to the settlement of Mayfield. You'll see a sign on the right indicating the entrance to Mayfield Falls. The road from the north passes through Flower Hill before you see the Original Mayfield sign on the left.

Paradise Park

Paradise Park (tel. 876/955-2675, paradise1@cwjamaica.com, US$40) is one of the best places in Jamaica for down-to-earth small-group rides on an expansive seaside cattle ranch located a few kilometers east of Savanna-la-Mar in Ferris Cross. Tours are offered for a maximum of 10 riders. The 1.5-hour ride covers diverse scenery, and the price includes complimentary soft drink, while lunch can be prepared for groups of six or more (US$12 per person). For those not interested in horseback riding, the park features a lovely picnic area with a barbecue

© OLIVER HILL

The beach at Paradise Park is among the few pristine stretches of white sand left in Jamaica.

grill, bathrooms, and a gentle river suitable for a refreshing dip (US$5).

Accommodations and Food

Blue Hole Garden (contact property manager cell tel. 876/401-5312) has a handful of basic cottages (US$40–50), the nicest of which, Lover's Nest, sits right over Roaring River. There is also a large house (US$80) up on the hill, which has a full kitchen and TV.

The Ranch Jerk Centre cooks up Boston-style jerk on the western side of Sav.

Sweet Spice (Barracks Rd., beside new bus park, tel. 876/955-3232, US$4.50–7.50) serves fried chicken, curry goat, oxtail, and fish fillet.

Devon House I Scream is at 104 Great George Street, across from the post office (tel. 876/918-1287, daily 11 A.M.–9 P.M. Mon.–Thurs., 11 A.M.–11 P.M. Fri.–Sun.).

Hammond's Pastry Place (18 Great George St., tel. 876/955-2870, 8 A.M.–6:30 P.M. Mon.–Fri., closing at 8:30 P.M. on Saturday) serves patties, cakes, and deli sandwiches.

Hot Spot Restaurant (23 Lewis St., contact manager Elaine Jagdath, cell tel. 848-6335, 7 A.M.–8 P.M. Mon.–Sat., US$2.25–4.50) serves local dishes like fried chicken and curry goat. It is perhaps more mediocre than hot, but good enough to fill your belly in a crunch.

One Blood Illusion Night Club, on the outskirts of town heading toward Ferris Cross and Cave, may be the most happening nightspot in Sav, typically open on weekend nights.

Services

Shopper's Choice Wholesales & Retail has three locations in Sav (Queen St., tel. 876/955-2702 or 876/955-9645; 12 Brooks Plaza, tel. 876/955-2936; and Llandilo Rd., tel. 876/918-0620 or 876/918-1482).

Del-Mar Laundromat is at 2 Queen Street (tel. 876/918-2105).

Carlene (tel. 876/955-8078, cell tel. 876/872-9080 or 876/378-7853) runs a spa at her home and is trained in deep tissue and Swedish massage and reflexology (US$60/

WESTERN CONSCIOUSNESS

Conscious Reggae is back in the limelight after nearly 20 years in the backseat – thanks to steadfast artists and promoters like Worrel King who have stood by the principles established by the genre's early pioneers. Starting around the time of Bob Marley's death in 1981, the reggae industry was taken over by dancehall artists like Shabba Ranks and Yellowman. The style of these artists' lyrics signified a departure from roots reggae, with its messages of truth and progress, to an often violent and sexually explicit form of music that became known as "slackness." When Peter Tosh was killed six years later in 1987, dancehall had taken over, and conscious reggae music was like yesterday's news. It was around that time that Worrel King founded King of Kings Promotions to try to rescue the truth from the mire.

King of Kings hit the ground running in 1988, organizing a very successful event at Titchfield High School in Port Antonio dubbed Eastern Consciousness, which showcased several artists, all of whom displayed some conscious leaning. "It was to attract people who needed to be uplifted, rather than just wasting away gyrating," King says. After a second successful Eastern Consciousness the following year, King took the event to Westmoreland, the parish of his birth, where he says the people were yearning for it. King describes his work as being guided by the hand of the Most High Jah, but says it has not been an easy road as consciousness is not something that sells easily. Nevertheless, the success of these early conscious stage shows has been mirrored in a multitude of other annual events inspired directly or indirectly by Eastern Consciousness. These include East Fest, held in Morant Bay and organized by Morgan Heritage,

and Rebel Salute, held at the Port Kaiser sports ground in Saint Elizabeth and organized by Tony Rebel. Both events have a decidedly "conscious" theme rarely challenged by the invited performers. "I look at artists that have been depicting consciousness," King says, "I don't look only at the hardcore consciousness, but at those who have the repertoire of conscious songs – even Beenie Man has a good 40-minute set that depicts consciousness – he performed at Western Consciousness as Ras Moses – it's not just those artists that are hardcore roots."

In 2006, King succeeded in bringing producer/performer extraordinaire Lee Scratch Perry back to Jamaica to perform for the first time in decades. King says he was termed a madman when he first suggested bringing Scratch home to perform, not any less given that many consider Scratch himself mad. After meeting with Scratch and his manager wife however, King said, "If he was mad that was the kind of madness I wanted to work with."

King has also created other concert events, including Tribute, dedicated to Peter Tosh. The free event held yearly in Sav's Independence Park is meant to showcase reggae sanity. In addition to the concert there is a Peter Tosh Symposium at the University of Westmoreland, which looks at the intellectual side of Peter Tosh and also highlights the work of other artists such as Burning Spear and Lee Scratch Perry. The event has drawn attendees from the highest levels, including finance minister Omar Davies, a self-proclaimed Tosh scholar. The Tribute concert is held on the Saturday closest to Peter Tosh's October 19 birthday, with the symposium held the previous Saturday.

---

hour). She can also be convinced to come to you if you're staying in the area.

WESTMORELAND INTERIOR
Beyond Mayfield Falls, which has grown into a favorite ecotourism attraction, the interior of Westmoreland sees few visitors. Nevertheless, there are a few notable cultural

and agricultural attractions, namely Seaford Town, reached via the South Coast from Ferris Cross.

Border Jerk (11 A.M.–10 P.M. daily, US$5–12), located in Mackfield, Westmoreland at the Hanover border along the B8 heading toward Montego Bay from Ferris Cross, is a notable jerk pit owned by Clive McFarlane (cell tel.

876/542-1852), who opened the business in 2004. It serves jerk chicken, pork, festival, and breadfruit. There's also a bar on-site.

Sights

Seaford Town is a cultural anomaly deep in the hills of Westmoreland. Founded in 1835 under a township act aimed at populating Jamaica's interior with Europeans, Seaford Town became the isolated home for 249 individuals transplanted from Germany. Jamaica's landed elite had feared the country's interior would be captured or settled by slaves, who were to be given full freedom in 1838. Baron Seaford thus allocated 202 hectares of his Montpelier Mountain Estate to the cause, and Jamaica's first German township was soon founded. The immigrants didn't find in Jamaica exactly what they had expected, however, and many died within the first weeks due to food shortages and their vulnerability to tropical diseases. The majority survived, however, adopting Jamaican food and customs and all but losing their connection to their homeland.

To this day many residents in Seaford Town have a light complexion, Catholicism is still an important religion, and some residents can still recall a few words of German. A small museum in the center of town features the area's unique history. The African Caribbean Institute recently launched a project called The Seaford Town Community History Project with support from the German Embassy to produce a comprehensive history of the community from 1835 to the present, including an audio documentation as part of the Jamaica Memory Bank (JMB).

To get to Seaford Town, head east in Mackfield toward Struie, continuing straight through Lambs River.

Bluefields and Belmont

This stretch of Westmoreland coast is as laid-back and "country" as Jamaica gets, with excellent accommodation options and plenty of seafood. Bluefields public beach has more locals on it than tourists, with shacks selling fried fish, beer, and the ubiquitous herb. The windfall of jobs and revenue that Butch Stewart and the Jamaican government were to bring to the area from the opening of another monstrous all-inclusive resort, Sandals Whitehouse, has hardly materialized, as the guests are not encouraged to venture off the compound and rarely do so.

History

The stretch of coast around Bluefields has a rich history. One of the three earliest Spanish settlements, named Oristan, which was initially based in Parottee, St. Elizabeth, and later moved to present-day Bluefields. Oristan was connected by road to Sevilla la Nueva, the Spanish capital just west of present-day St. Ann's Bay, as well as to Santiago de la Vega, in present-day Spanish Town. The area was favored by the Spanish under early colonial rule, and later, the pirate Henry Morgan departed from Bluefields Bay to sack Panama in 1670. Still later, it was the spot Captain Bligh landed after finally successfully completing his charge of bringing breadfruit to the island from Tahiti. What is said to be the original breadfruit tree in Jamaica was taken down by Hurricane Ivan in 2004 and sits in a pile of cut-up pieces on one side of the lawn at **Bluefields Great House.** Pimento, or allspice as it's known in many places, was an important cash crop in the area, at some point having been replaced by marijuana in importance for the local economy.

SIGHTS

Bluefields Beach is a popular local hangout and sees very few tourists. It has fine white sand and is lined with vendors. Music is often blasted on weekends when the beach fills up.

Bluefields Great House, located about 0.4 kilometer inland from the police station, on the road to Brighton, was the home of many of the area's most distinguished temporary inhabitants, including Philip Henry Goss, an English ornithologist who resided in Jamaica 1844–1846, subsequently completing the work *Birds of Jamaica, a Naturalist's Sojourn in Jamaica.*

The **Peter Tosh Memorial Garden,** where the remains of this original Wailer lie, is worth a quick stop, if only to pause amid the ganja seedlings to remember one of the world's greatest reggae artists. An entrance fee is assessed (US$5) when there's someone around to collect it. Otherwise the gate is unlocked and a quick visit usually goes unnoticed. In mango season the yard is full of locals fighting over the heavily laden branches. Peter Tosh was born in nearby Grange Hill before

making his way to Kingston, where he became one of the original three Wailers along with Bob Marley and Bunny Livingston. His mother still lives in Belmont.

RECREATION

The Bluefields area is the perfect place for activities like hiking, swimming, snorkeling, and relaxing. Nobody is touting parasailing or Jet Skis, and the most activity you will see on the water are catamarans crossing Parker's Bay off the Culloden shoreline from Sandals Whitehouse. There's a good horseback riding operation within a 15-minute drive at the expansive beachside **Paradise Park** estate (tel. 876/955-2675, paradise1@cwjamaica. com, US$40 per person) to the west in Ferris Cross.

ACCOMMODATIONS
Under US$100

Brian Wedderburn has a **Roots Cottage** (cell tel. 876/384-6610, US$30) at his yard in

Bluefields Beach is the most utilized public beach on the South Coast, where residents of Belmont and Bluefields spend many a Sunday.

Belmont with a little fridge, fan, and bathroom with cold water.

Belmont Garden Cottages (contact Damian "Juicy" Forrester, cell tel. 876/425-2387 or tel. 876/955-8143, US$30) has six cottages, with private baths, one with hot water. All have standing fans, TV, stove, fridge, and microwave.

《 Rainbow Villas (tel. 876/955-8078, cell tel. 876/872-9080 or 876/378-7853, info@rainbowvillas-jamaica.com or rainbowvillas@cwjamaica.com, www.rainbowvillas-jamaica.com, US$25 s, US$45 d), owned and managed by the stunning Carlene and her German husband Ralph, is located across the road from the water along a little lane adjacent to Sunset Paradise Bar & Grill. The spacious and clean rooms have ceiling fans and kitchenettes, hot water, and air-conditioning. Carlene has a spa on property specializing in deep tissue and Swedish massage and reflexology (US$60/hour).

US$100-250

Shafston Great House (contact Frank Lohmann, cell tel. 876/869-9212, mail@shafston.com, www.shafston.com) is one of the few plantation great houses that you can actually stay in. Set on a hill overlooking Bluefields Bay, Shafston has a large pool and rooms that range from basic with shared bath (US$140 d) in the side building, to suites in the Great House with hot water in private baths (US$180 d). Rates include meals and drinks. Frank also offers transfers from the airport in Mobay (US$75).

《 Horizon Cottages (cell tel. 876/382-6384, info@barrettadventures.com, www.carolynscaribbeancottages.com, US$110, three-night minimum stay, fourth night is free) define rustic elegance, with two perfectly situated wooden cottages on Bluefields Bay. Each cottage is tastefully decorated with local artwork and has classic wooden louvered windows, queen-size beds, soft linens, attached bath with private outdoor showers, and cute, functional kitchens. The porch steps of **Sea Ranch** descend onto the small and beautiful private white-sand beach, and a pier off

the manicured lawn makes the perfect dining room and cocktail bar. **Rasta Ranch** is a slightly larger cottage set farther back in the yard. Kayaks and snorkeling gear are on-hand for excursions to the reef just offshore. Property manager Carolyn Barrett is a seasoned tour operator who runs Barrett Adventures, one of the island's best outfits, and can accommodate the interests of every kind of adventure seeker. Horizon's main house was the first built on the waterfront in the area. Wireless Internet, hot water, and gentle lapping waves make Horizon a very hard place to leave. The property owners also control Blue Hole Garden on Roaring River, 20 minutes to the west.

Over US$250

Bluefields Villas (tel. 202/232-4010, fax 703/549-6517, vacations@bluefieldsvillas.com, www.bluefieldsvillas.com) are easily the area's most luxurious accommodation option, and among the most scrupulously maintained villas in Jamaica. If you've ever had the desire to feel like royalty, there is no better place than **The Hermitage** (US$5,600/8,400 weekly low/high season). Antique furniture and four-poster beds, seamlessly integrated with the classic design of the spacious villa, seem to have been specially created for a neocolonialist emperor. A large sundeck off the dining room looks over the sea, while the next dining room door opens over a tiled pool. The "silent butler" is never far off to deliver anything you might require, and delicious food is served at mealtimes with the utmost attention to presentation and form.

San Michele (a Bluefields Villas property), 1.5 kilometers down the coast, is another gorgeous villa from the set. It has a small island perfect for enjoying the area's spectacular sunsets with cocktail in hand, connected to the lawn by a narrow bridge.

FOOD

Judge Beer Joint (just west of Kd's, tel. 876/385-5184), run by Eugene "Judge"

NEGRIL

© OLIVER HILL

The Hermitage is among the finest villas in Jamaica, with impeccable service and unparalleled sea vistas.

Stephenson, serves steamed or roast fish (US$6–7/lb.), and fish tea (US$1 per cup).

Sunset Paradise Bar & Grill (across from Kd's, tel. 876/955-8164) is owned by Quashi and serves drinks around a nice rustic bar, as well as Jamaican staples like stewed chicken (US$3). Quashi's cousin Patrice can usually be found behind the bar.

Kd's Fish Pot (on the water 50 meters east of the Peter Tosh Memorial Garden) has been in business since 1973. Opening hours are not regular. Kd died in 2008, but his girlfriend still runs the place and cooks in the afternoons, depending on supply of fish and demand from customers. A small stage setup on the waterfront is sometimes used for events.

Fresh Touch Restaurant (Bluefields Beach Park, contact owner Otis Wright, cell tel. 876/870-6303, or manager Pearl Stephenson, cell tel. 876/357-0875, 6:30 A.M.–10 P.M. daily) serves steamed, roasted, and fried fish, as well as other coastal staples like fish tea, lobster, fried chicken, and curry goat, all served with a side of rice and peas. On Sundays and holidays Bluefields Beach Park is the most happening scene on the South Coast.

WHITEHOUSE

A quiet seaside community, Whitehouse has developed into a favored community for Jamaicans returning after years of working abroad, thanks to a few developers who've built subdivisions and sold off lots and homes. The nicest beach in the area, Whitehouse Beach, was cordoned off and annexed by the last Sandals to be built in Jamaica.

Recreation

Brian "Bush Doctor" Wedderburn (cell tel. 876/384-6610), also known locally as Rasta Brian, leads **hiking excursions** (US$10 per person) into the hills to learn about local flora and fauna.

Fishing excursions can be organized by Lagga or Trevor, who can be contacted through Carolyn Barrett, manager of Horizon Cottages and owner of Barrett Adventures (tel. 876/382-6384, info@barrettadventures.com).

Reliable Adventures Jamaica (tel. 876/955-8834, cell tel. 876/421-7449, wolde99@yahoo.com, www.jamaicabirding.com) organizes community tours as well as birding, hiking, and marine excursions with local fisherman, led by Wolde Kristos. One-day bird tours run US$85 per person including lunch.

Accommodations

Natania's (tel. 876/963-5349, cell tel. 876/883-3009, nataniasjamaica@yahoo.com, www.nataniasjamaica.com, US$80–100) is run B&B-style with eight double-occupancy rooms, some facing inland, the others out to sea. Rooms have either two single beds or one king-size. Owner Veronica Probst took the name Natania from the names of her two daughters, Natalie and Tania. Veronica has run the place since 1983. The property sits on the waterfront overlooking Parker's Bay. Food is prepared to order. Amenities include direct TV, a pool, and sandy ocean access with a seaside gazebo.

Culloden by the Sea is a large subdivision development just west of Whitehouse. Several repatriated Jamaicans have built houses there to retire to and a few of them rent as nice, low-key guesthouses. **Sierra-la-Mar Villa** (Lot #150, Culloden-by-the-Sea, contact Garth Lee at tel. 876/963-5922, cell tel. 876/841-2299, garthlee1@cwjamaica.com, www.sierralamar.com, US$1,790 weekly for up to 12 people or US$900 weekly for exclusive rental of the entire house for two guests) is a nice six-bedroom villa perched high on the hill overlooking Whitehouse. Sierra-la-Mar has a three-day minimum year-round. Amenities include satellite TV, washer/dryer, fully equipped kitchen, air-conditioning in bedrooms, private pool and deck with a beautiful view, and Wi-Fi.

FantaSea (Culloden by the Sea, contact manager Marcia Laird, cell tel. 876/383-5347, or owner Rudy Miller, U.S. tel. 973/214-1423, www.fantaseavilla.com, US$1,600 weekly for up to four adults) is a five-bedroom, four-bath hilltop villa with a little swimming pool, a wrap-around kitchen bar/counter, and verandas that take full advantage of the breathtaking

PEDRO BANK AND PEDRO CAYS

Nearly 100 kilometers offshore south of Bluefields Bay, the Pedro Cays form the surface of the Pedro Bank, one of Jamaica's few remaining unspoiled marine ecosystems. The Pedro Bank is a submerged mass about three quarters the size of mainland Jamaica, one of the largest banks in the Caribbean Basin, and provides a habitat for queen conch, which has historically been one of Jamaica's most important exports. Increased fishing is threatening the bank however, and an international conservation effort is underway to protect the unique marine habitat. Fishermen leave from points all along the South Coast for extended periods on the cays, usually returning with a lucrative catch to bring to market.

views. The villa can sleep a maximum of 12 people with a US$100 per week surcharge added for each additional adult. Bedrooms have air-conditiong, and the villa has internet and offers unlimited calls to the U.S. and Canada.

Ocean Air Guest House (84 South Sea Park Drive, contact owner/manager Marcia Palmer, tel. 876/389-9155, oceanairguesthouse@yahoo.com, US$43–71) has eight standard rooms and a suite with four queen-size beds. Rooms have queen-size beds, air-conditioning, and local TV. The pool overlooks the waterfront, and there is a small beach below the house. Meals can be arranged to order (US$5–20/person).

South Sea View Guest House (tel. 876/963-5172, run by Norman Forrester, cell tel. 876/404-6040, southseaview@yahoo.com, www.southseaviewjamaica.com, US$75–85) is a seaside guest house with king-size beds, air-conditioning, TV, and private bath. Much of the food served in the restaurant is grown on Norman's organic farm.

Sandals Whitehouse (U.S. tel. 800/726-3257, starting at US$790) took about 15 years to complete at a total cost of around US$110 million—among the most expensive hotels ever built and nearly double the initial budget estimates. At the high end of Sandals' many properties island-wide, the four-star Sandals Whitehouse features premium drinks, a variety of dining options, and a beautiful cabaret bar. Rooms have all the amenities you could ask for. The property is stunningly grand, designed like a European village with a large central courtyard and enormous pool with a wet bar. The beach is one of the best in the area. Day passes (US$85, good until 6 P.M.) and evening passes (US$80, 6 P.M.–2 A.M.) are also available, and the hotel also offers a full-day pass (US$130, 10 A.M.–2 A.M.). There's a two-night minimum stay.

Culloden Cove (contact Andy McLean, tel. 876/472-4608, info@jamaica-holidayvilla.com, www.jamaicaholidayvilla.com, US$2,660–3,100 weekly low season, US$2,975–3,745 high season), located at the former home of the Culloden Café, received a complete refurbishment under new ownership in 2008, leaving the property in the immaculate condition of a top-notch villa. The property sleeps up to 10, six in the villa and four in a separate cottage. An infinity pool is located seaside, at the bottom of a sloping lawn extending from the main house, with a gazebo at the water's edge.

Food
Box Video Rental and Cook Shop (Whitehouse Square, cell tel. 876/363-0091, 9 A.M.–3 P.M. daily, rent videos until 8 P.M.; food US$2–4) is a great food joint run out of a shipping container by enterprising Raquel "Keisha" Smith. Chicken and pork dishes come in three sizes. Fish is also cooked when it's available.

Ruby's 24/7 (Whitehouse Square, tel. 876/453-0003) serves typical Jamaican dishes around the clock, in a box to go or to stay.

Becky's (8:30 A.M.–11 P.M. Mon.–Sat., US$3–6), located about 100 meters farther west, serves typical Jamaican dishes like oxtail, fish, pork, curry goat, and fried chicken, as well as burgers and fries.

Jimmyz Restaurant and Bar (tel. 876/390-3477, Mon.–Sat. 6 A.M.–7 P.M., US$3.50–11) located at the local fishing beach and run by George "Jimmy" Williams, serves Jamaican breakfast items like ackee and saltfish accompanied by yam and boiled banana, with lunch and dinner dishes that include chicken and seafood staples. Fresh juices are also served.

Getting There and Around
Route taxis ply the coast all day long from Sav-la-Mar (US$2) and Black River (US$2) to Whitehouse. Karl (cell tel. 876/368-0508) is a JUTA-licensed driver based in the area who offers tours and taxi service.

MONTEGO BAY AND THE NORTHWEST

Montego Bay is the capital of St. James parish. Commonly referred to by locals as "Mobay," it's a place buzzing with cruise ships and international flights brimming with tourists. Many of these tourists spend barely a day on land before climbing aboard to depart for the next port. Others stay with their families in private villas for months of the year. Mobay's bustling service economy serves a large middle class, many of who spend much of the year abroad. This contrasts with large squatter settlements and an urban squalor that permeates the downtown area. On the quiet peninsula of Freeport, the city has an active yacht club, whose members partake in exciting events throughout the year; world-class golf courses lie east and west of the city. It's little wonder that many hotels register high occupancy throughout much of the year. Yet because the economy is overwhelmingly dependent on tourism, there arises at times a tangible resentment between the local population, a proud lot with fiery roots steeped in a not-so-distant, brutal history, and the endless flow of transient visitors, often perceived as cogs in the local economic machinery. But the congested angst of downtown Mobay quickly dissipates beyond the city limits, where the landscape of rural St. James quickly transforms into forested hills traversed by the occasional river.

The bordering parish to the east along the North Coast is Trelawny, seemingly still reminiscing over a glorious but languished past when Falmouth, its ornate capital, had money and class. As sugar lost importance

© OLIVER HILL

MONTEGO BAY

HIGHLIGHTS

◖ **Richmond Hill:** With the best view over Mobay – and a hotel, bar, and restaurant rich in history and ambience – this is a choice spot for a sunset cocktail (page 59).

◖ **Gallery of West Indian Art:** Not only does it have an excellent collection of Jamaican work, but there are Cuban and Haitian paintings as well (page 60).

◖ **Rose Hall Great House:** There's perhaps no great house as ominous and grand, and the spirit of White Witch Annie Palmer can still be felt (page 62).

◖ **Greenwood Great House:** One of the most beautiful and true-to-its-day estate

houses in Jamaica, it played a central role in the island's sugar history (page 62).

◖ **Doctors Cave Beach:** Center stage on Mobay's Hip Strip, this is the best spot to see and be seen on weekends. It's also the site of monthly full-moon parties (page 64).

◖ **Falmouth:** Considered one of the world's best examples of a Georgian town, it's changed little from its boom years at the height of the island's sugar trade (page 83).

◖ **Queen of Spain Valley:** Home to a 810-hectare citrus plantation, ceramics studio, and luxury retreat, it's worth every bit of bad road covered on the way (page 91).

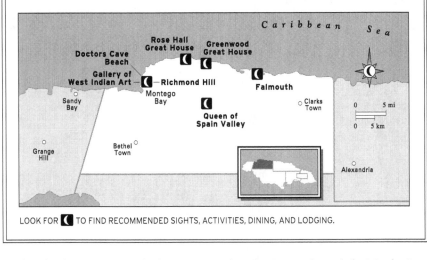

LOOK FOR ◖ TO FIND RECOMMENDED SIGHTS, ACTIVITIES, DINING, AND LODGING.

in the island's economy in the late 1800s, Falmouth faded from preeminent port to sleepy backwater. Today the parish is slowly showing signs of rejuvenation as the world begins to acknowledge its architectural treasures, with international funding being successfully sourced and funneled by local NGO Falmouth Heritage Renewal. Trelawny boomed during the years of the sugar trade but was an important strategic area even before the time of parishes—going back to

when the Spaniards used the Martha Brae River as a thoroughfare to traverse the island from the South to North Coasts. Their first major settlement of Melilla is said to have been near the mouth of the river. Before the Spaniards, the Martha Brae was the lifeblood for the area's Taino population, whose surviving legends are evidence of the river's importance to them.

Cockpit Country occupies the interior between the North and South Coasts, covering

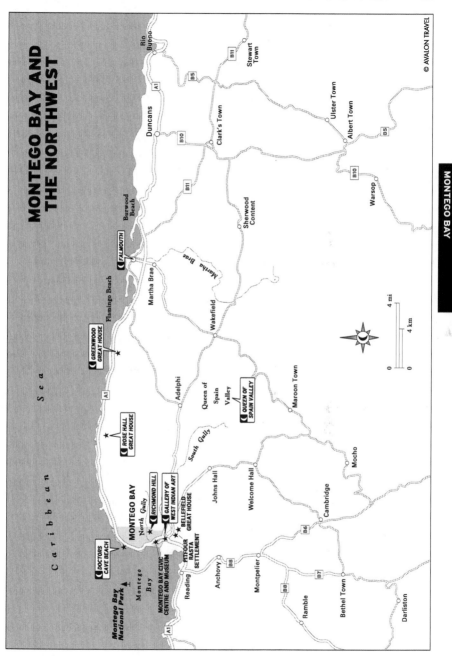

MONTEGO BAY AND
THE NORTHWEST

Caribbean Sea

© AVALON TRAVEL

MONTEGO BAY

some of the most rugged terrain in the world, where limestone sinkholes, craggy hillocks, countless caves, and underground rivers made pursuit of Jamaica's Maroons a difficult task for the British colonists attempting to establish order and dominion. Together with the island's mountainous northeast, Trelawny gave respite to the indomitable Maroons; the parish remains a Maroon stronghold and adventurers' paradise. At the same time, the parish has the most peaceful and romantic farmlands in Jamaica, the Queen of Spain Valley being a particularly beautiful crown jewel amidst rough, rounded hilltops, where a citrus plantation today stands on the sugar estate of yesteryear. Cruising on horseback through this part of Jamaica is exhilarating and timelessly romantic, with orange and coconut groves and picturesque misty hills making for breathtaking scenery. This parish is rarely explored by tourists beyond the coastal areas of Falmouth, the Luminous Lagoon, and the Martha Brae River. As remote as Trelawny may seem when deep inside a cave or otherwise immersed in the bush, you are never more than a couple hours from civilization, or some semblance of it, in Montego Bay.

PLANNING YOUR TIME

Given the proximity of Negril, Jamaica's most developed beach town, as well as the mountains of the Dolphin Head range in Hanover, the interior and South Coast of neighboring Westmoreland, and Cockpit Country in St. James and Trelawny, there are plenty of opportunities for recreation and relaxation from a base in Montego Bay without being on the road for more than a couple hours. Closer to town there are several estate great house tours and plantation tours that make excellent half-day outings. Should you wish to hit the beach, there are plenty of options right

in town, while Trelawny also has its share of good beaches.

Mobay makes a convenient base thanks to Sangster International Airport on the eastern side of town. As a point of entry, Mobay is probably the best option, and a night or two in the city, especially if you arrive on the weekend, can be a good way to catch the Jamaican vibe before heading off to a more tranquil corner of the island. But Mobay shouldn't be the only area you visit on a trip to Jamaica. Ideally the area deserves around five days, splitting your time between the beach or another natural attraction, and a visit to a historical site, with some fine dining around the city.

Historical places of interest include Sam Sharpe Square in downtown Mobay, Bellefield, Rose Hall and Greenwood great houses—at least one of which should be seen on a trip to Jamaica—and the Georgian town of Falmouth. All of these make good half-day visits, while Falmouth can easily consume the better part of an unhurried day. Natural attractions in the region include the Martha Brae River, Cockpit Country caves, Mayfield Falls, the Great River, and a handful of working plantations that offer tours. Organized tour operators on the western side of Jamaica usually include transportation to and from Montego Bay or Negril hotels. A few decent beaches along the Hip Strip, on Dead End Road, and at the resorts farther east along the coast make Mobay a good place to hang out and catch some sun, but the city is by no means the place to go for secluded stretches of sand or unspoiled wilderness.

A few times a year, Mobay comes alive for music festivals that are, for many people, reason enough to travel to Jamaica. These include the island's premier music festival, Reggae Sumfest, held in July, and Jazz and Blues Festival (www.jamaicajazzandblues.com), held each January.

Montego Bay

Jamaica's "vibes city," Mobay has been the principal hub of the island's tourism industry since the 1950s, with the country's most well-heeled duty-free shops and beaches. The close proximity of the area's hotels to the Montego Bay airport makes it a convenient destination for long-weekenders visiting from the United States and those looking to take advantage of the proximity of destinations on the western side of the island. Sangster International Airport receives most of Jamaica's three million annual tourists, and the surrounding region offers plenty of activities for day trips out of town, making the Mobay area the most popular place for visitors to Jamaica to find lodging. But the picture is not entirely pretty, and plenty of strife plagues the city, not least of which derives from growing squatter communities in and around town. Many visitors find in Montegonians, also known as "bawn a bays," a hard-edged, matter-of-fact idiosyncrasy that reflects the dual worlds coexisting in the energetic city. Perhaps a tumultuous history kept fresh by perpetuating injustices leads the city's inhabitants to despise the subservience inherent in a tourism-based economy out of pride, even if it is tourism that sustains the town. Montego Bay has been at the center of the island's economic picture since the days of the Spanish, and it is not lost on the local population that the city remains an economic powerhouse with its booming service economy.

Old timers recall the golden years of 1960s Mobay, when clubs like the Yellow Bird on Church Street, Club 35 on Union Street, and Cats Corner were brimming with tourists and locals alike. Taxis would carry guests from the hotels to the city center, where they would await patrons into the early morning hours to emerge from smoky cabarets bursting with live music. The Michael Manley era, which began in 1972, ushered in a socialism scare that destabilized Jamaica, affecting the tourism market directly with travel advisories warning would-be visitors to stay away. Nowhere was the impact more severe than in Montego Bay, which was the most-developed resort destination in Jamaica at the time. It was during the 1970s that all-inclusive tourism became a phenomenon, and gated resorts became the norm. The overwhelming dominance of all-inclusive hotels in recent years has led fewer visitors to leave the hotel compounds to explore the city, stifling business for restaurants and bars, more successful of which cater as much to the local market as to tourists. Today Mobay comes alive on certain nights of the week and gets especially lively for several notable annual festivals, like Jazz and Blues Festival and Reggae Sumfest.

Commercially Montego Bay is organized like many U.S. cities. Large shopping centers dot the urban landscape, with KFC and Burger King dominating two strong poles of the quasi-modern city—only quasi-modern because Mobay contains in a small space some of Jamaica's roughest areas (there have been weeks in recent memory that saw several police-inflicted killings in some of Mobay's worse districts). But along Mobay's Hip Strip in the vicinity of Doctors Cave, Cornwall, and Dead End Beaches, the mood is as outwardly genteel as during the early British colonial period.

Mobay has been crucial to the island since the arrival of the Spanish conquistadores. The name Montego is said to have its origin in the Spanish word *manteca* (lard), referring to the use of the bay as an export center for wild hog products, namely lard. The city was previously named Golfo de Buen Tiempo (Bay of Good Weather) by Christopher Columbus.

Orientation

Montego Bay has distinct tourist zones, well separated from the bustling and raucous downtown area. The main tourist area is the **Hip Strip** along Gloucester Avenue, where most of the bars, restaurants, and hotels catering to tourists are located. Extending off the strip is **Kent Avenue**, a.k.a. Dead End Road, which

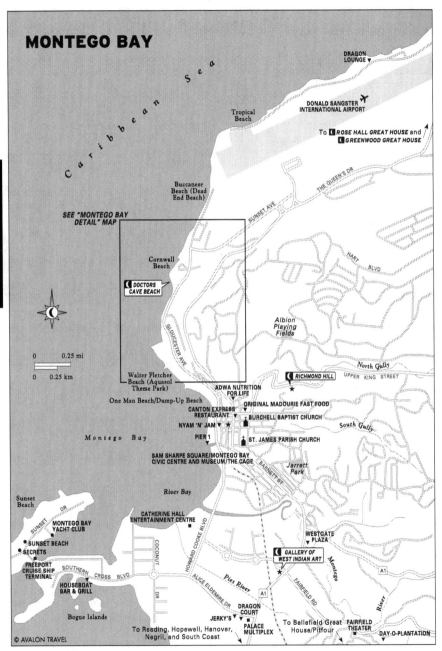

MONTEGO BAY

C a r i b b e a n   S e a

DRAGON LOUNGE ▼

DONALD SANGSTER INTERNATIONAL AIRPORT ✈

Tropical Beach

To **C**ROSE HALL GREAT HOUSE and **C**GREENWOOD GREAT HOUSE

THE QUEEN'S DR

Buccaneer Beach (Dead End Beach)

SUNSET AVE

SEE "MONTEGO BAY DETAIL" MAP

HART BLVD

Cornwall Beach

C DOCTORS CAVE BEACH

Albion Playing Fields

0   0.25 mi
0   0.25 km

GLOUCESTER AVE

North Gully

C RICHMOND HILL ★
UPPER KING STREET

Walter Fletcher Beach (Aquasol Theme Park)

ADWA NUTRITION FOR LIFE ★

One Man Beach/Dump-Up Beach

ORIGINAL MADOURIE FAST FOOD ▼

CANTON EXPRESS RESTAURANT ▼
NYAM 'N' JAM ▼ ★
PIER 1 ▼

+ BURCHELL BAPTIST CHURCH

South Gully

Montego   Bay

⌂ ST. JAMES PARISH CHURCH

SAM SHARPE SQUARE/MONTEGO BAY CIVIC CENTRE AND MUSEUM/THE CAGE

Jarrett Park

BARNETT ST

River Bay

Sunset Beach

CATHERINE HALL ENTERTAINMENT CENTRE ■

SUNSET DR

MONTEGO BAY YACHT CLUB

● SUNSET BEACH
● SECRETS

FREEPORT CRUISE SHIP TERMINAL

SOUTHERN   CROSS   BLVD

HOUSEBOAT BAR & GRILL

HOWARD COOKE BLVD

COCONUT

WESTGATE PLAZA

C GALLERY OF WEST INDIAN ART ★

Montego

A1

COCONUT DR

ALICE ELDEMIRE DR

Pies River

A1

FAIRFIELD RD

River

Bogue Islands

To Reading, Hopewell, Hanover, Negril, and South Coast

JERKY'S ▼

DRAGON COURT

PALACE MULTIPLEX

To Bellefield Great House/Pitfour

FAIRFIELD THEATER

DAY-O-PLANTATION

© AVALON TRAVEL

terminates at the end of the airport runway. **Queens Drive** passes along the hill above the Hip Strip with several budget hotels, many of them frequented by locals seeking privacy with their special someone.

Downtown Montego Bay is centered on **Sam Sharpe Square,** where a statue of the slave rebellion leader stands in one corner. The peninsula of **Freeport** sticks out into the Bogue Lagoon and the Montego Bay Marine Park just west of downtown, with the cruise ship terminal, the yacht club, Sunset Beach and Secrets resorts located there.

East of the airport, Ironshore is a middle class area that covers a large swath of hill in subdivisions and oversized concrete houses. East of Ironshore, Spring Garden is the most exclusive residential neighborhood in Mobay, bordering Rose Hall Estate where many of the area's all-inclusive resorts are wedged between the main road and the sea. Half Moon Resort, the Ritz Carlton, and Palmyra are the most luxurious of Mobay's accommodation options. Also nearby is Rose Hall Resort (a Hilton hotel), Sea Castles, a former resort now rented as apartment units, and three Iberostar hotels in a large complex a few kilometers further to the east down the coast.

SIGHTS
◖ Richmond Hill

Whether or not you choose to stay at this gorgeous hilltop property, a sunset cocktail from the beautiful poolside terrace will remain a romantic memory indefinitely.

The hotel has an illustrious history. Columbus apparently stayed here for a year while he was stranded in Jamaica, and it was once part of Annie Palmer's Rose Hall Estate. Later, in 1838, the property was acquired and built into a palatial abode by the Dewar family of Scotch whisky fame. Today the hotel is owned and operated with charm by Stefanie Chin and daughters Gracie and Gale, Austrian expatriates in Jamaica since 1968.

Montego Bay Marine Park

Montego Bay Marine Park (tel. 876/952-5619, contact@mbmp.org, www.mbmp.org) consists

of the entire bay from high-tide mark on land to 100-meter depth from Reading on Mobay's western edge, to just east of the airport on the eastern side. The marine park encompasses diverse ecosystems that include mangrove forests, islands, beaches, estuaries, sea-grass beds, and corals. The best way to see the marine park is with a licensed tour operator for a snorkeling trip or with a glass-bottomed boat tour. Tropical Beach and Aquasol both operate glass-bottomed boat tours, with the former including snorkeling.

Pitfour Rasta Settlement

Pitfour (contact Sister Norma, cell tel. 876/882-6376) is a Rastafarian settlement in the Granville district in the hills above Montego Bay. A Nyabinghi ceremony lasting more than a week begins every November 1 to celebrate the coronation of His Imperial Majesty Haile Selassie I, revered by Rastafarians as their God. On Good Friday of every year, a Nyabinghi vigil known as the Coral Gardens Groundation is held to commemorate the murder of Rastafarians by the Jamaican authorities in the early years of the movement. When events are held, Rastas come from across Jamaica to participate. Otherwise the settlement is very sleepy, with little happening beyond perhaps a reasoning between *bredren* over a burning chalice. To get to Pitfour head inland from Catherine Hall along Fairfield Road, taking a right after the Fairfield Theatre, passing Day-O Plantation. Take the first right after the police station in the square, then continue straight, and then take the first left in Granville. By the gate to Pitfour you will see Bongo Manny and Daughter Norma Ital food shop.

Montego Bay Civic Centre and Museum

Mobay's Civic Center (Sam Sharpe Square, tel. 876/971-9417, 9 A.M.–5 P.M. Mon.–Fri., US$2 adults, US$0.75 children) houses a museum featuring a history of St. James. The small collection of artifacts spans the Taino period to the present day. The museum is under the management of the Institute of Jamaica, with assistant curator Leanne Rodney offering 30-minute tours throughout the day. Arrangements can

be made for the museum to be open on weekends for 10 or more visitors by calling during the week to make a request.

The Cage, also in Sam Sharpe Square, was once used to lock up misbehaving slaves and sailors.

St. James Parish Church (Church St., tel. 876/971-2564) is one of the most attractive buildings in town. It's set amongst large grounds that house a small cemetery.

Burchell Baptist Church (Market St., tel. 876/971-9141) is a more humble church where Sam Sharpe used to preach. His remains are interred there.

◖ Gallery of West Indian Art

The Gallery of West Indian Art (11 Fairfield Rd., Catherine Hall, tel. 876/952-4547, nikola@cwjamaica.com, www.galleryofwestindianart.com) is one of the most diverse galleries in Jamaica—as far as carrying both Jamaican art and pieces from neighboring islands, especially Haiti and Cuba. The gallery is owned and operated by Nicki and Steffan, who make

Locals take cover from a light rain outside the Montego Bay Civic Centre in Sam Sharpe Square.

SAM SHARPE, NATIONAL HERO

Sam Sharpe was the central figure of the Christmas Rebellion of 1831-1832, which many point to as the beginning of the end of slavery in Jamaica (officially granted in 1838). Sharpe was a Baptist deacon, well respected across the deep societal divides. Despite this, Sharpe was executed in a public hanging on May 23, 1832, in what is now Sam Sharpe Square in the heart of Montego Bay. Over 300 slaves were also executed for their role in the rebellion. Sharpe had originally envisioned and promoted a peaceful rebellion of passive resistance, whereby the slaves would stage a sit-down strike until the planters agreed to pay them for their labor, in accordance with what was perceived as a royal decree from England being withheld in Jamaica. The rebelling slaves were swept up in the excitement of the hour, however, as Sharpe's lieutenants swept across the western parishes to the sound of war drums belting out from the slave villages. Only 16 white people were killed during the rebellion, but around 20 large estates were torched, and the rebellion struck fear into the heart of the "plantocracy." Sharpe took responsibility for the rebellion, relieving the white missionaries of the blame that was focused on them by the established powers of the day, including the Anglican Church (which with few isolated and notable exceptions backed the landed elite, even organizing terror squads to target the Baptist missionaries who had made it their charge to foment discontent among the slaves). The Christmas Rebellion was consequently also known as the Baptist War.

quality pieces accessible with very reasonable pricing. Look out for work by Jamaican artists Delores Anglin and Gene Pearson, a sculptor specializing in bronze heads.

Mount Zion

Mount Zion is a quaint community that overlooks Rose Hall, with excellent panoramic views of the coast northeast of Mobay. A small church forms the centerpiece of the village, where views over Cinnamon Hill Golf Course and along the coast of Iron Shore and Rose Hall are unmatched. To get to Mount Zion, turn inland on an uncommonly well-paved road (no name) just past the small bridge that crosses Little River heading east from the Ritz-Carlton. The road heads up a steep hill toward the community of Cornwall. As the hill tapers off toward the top, a right turn leads farther up to the community of Zion Hill. Heading straight at the junction leads to Cornwall.

ESTATE GREAT HOUSES

Each of the area's estate great houses is worth visiting and quite distinct from the others. A visit to one or all of these historic properties is like traveling back in time—a great way to catch a glimpse of the island's glorious and tumultuous past.

Bellefield Great House

Bellefield Great House (tel. 876/952-2382, www.bellefieldgreathouse.com), five minutes from Mobay at Barnett Estate, offers a lunch tour Wednesdays and Thursdays (10:30 A.M.–2 P.M., US$40). It consists of a 45-minute visit through the great house and gardens, and a one-hour lunch serving well-prepared Jamaican dishes. The tour can be arranged on any day of the week for parties of 10 people or more. A basic tour, without the delicious lunch, is also offered (US$20). Bellefield belongs to the Kerr-Jarretts, a family that at one point controlled much of the land in and around Mobay as part of Fairfield Estate. The tour is operated by Nicky and David Farquharson, who are also behind the production of the exquisite meal. To get to Bellefield, take Fairfield Road from Catherine Hall, staying right where the road splits on to Chambers Drive until you reach the Granville Police Station. Take a right on Bellefield Road at the police station and go until you see the great house on the left.

Rose Hall Great House

Rose Hall Great House (tel. 876/953-2323, greathouse@rosehall.com, www.rosehall.com, US$20 adults, US$10 children) is the former home of Annie Palmer, remembered as the White Witch of Rose Hall in Herbert De Lisser's novel of the same name. It's the most formidable and foreboding estate great house on the island today, with a bone-chilling history behind its grandeur. The tour through the impeccably refurbished mansion is excellent. Rose Hall was built in 1770 by John Palmer, who ruled the estate with his wife, Rosa. The property passed through many hands before ending up in possession of John Rose Palmer, who married the infamous Annie in 1820. A slight woman not more than five feet tall, Annie is said to have practiced voodoo, or black magic, and would eventually kill several husbands and lovers, starting with Mr. John Rose. Annie ruled the plantation brutally and was much feared by the estate's slaves. She would ultimately taste her own medicine, as she was killed during the Christmas Rebellion of 1831 (which pushed England one step closer to the abolition of slavery).

Rose Hall was virtually abandoned with the decline in the sugar economy until an American rags-to-riches businessman, John Rollins, bought the estate in the 1960s and restored the great house to its old grandeur. Today the estate is governed by Mrs. Rollins, who has upheld the ambitious development ethic of her late husband. Rose Hall Great House forms the historic centerpiece of the vast Rose Hall Estate, which encompasses three 18-hole golf courses, the Ritz-Carlton, Half Moon and Rose Hall resorts, and the most desirable residential district of Montego Bay, Spring Farms. Also on the Rose Hall Estate, Cinnamon Hill Great House was the home of the late Johnny Cash. Cinnamon Hill is not currently open to the public except for special events.

Greenwood Great House

Greenwood Great House (tel. 876/953-1077, greenwoodgreathouse@cwjamaica.com, www.

greenwoodgreathouse.com, 9 A.M.–5 P.M. daily, US$14) is the best example of a great house kept alive by the owners, Bob and Ann Betton, who live on property and manage the low-key tour operation. Built in the late 1600s by one of the wealthiest families of the British colonial period, the Barretts first landed in Jamaica on Cromwell's voyage of conquest, when the island was captured from the Spanish in 1655. Land grants immediately made the family a major landholder, and its plantations grew over the next 179 years to amass 2,000 slaves on seven estates by the time of emancipation. Greenwood Great House boasted the best stretch of road in Jamaica as its driveway. Little upkeep has been performed over the past four centuries, apparently, and today the 1.5-kilometer-long road requires slow going, but the panoramic view from the house and grounds are still as good as ever.

Interesting relics like hand-pump fire carts and old wagon wheels adorn the outside of the building. Inside the house is the best collection of colonial-era antiques in Jamaica, including obscure musical instruments, Flemish thrones, and desks with secret compartments from the 17th century. An inlaid rosewood piano belonged to King Edward VII, and a portrait of poet Elizabeth Barrett Browning's cousin hangs on the wall. Another historical treasure at the great house is the will of Reverend Thomas Burchell, who was arrested for his alleged role in the Christmas Rebellion.

Farther inland from Greenwood lie the ruins of Barrett Hall, the family's primary residence.

Bob Marley School of the Arts Institute (Flamingo Beach, Ras Astor Black, cell tel. 876/327-9991, tel. 876/861-5233, or 847/571-5804, astor@bobartsinstitute.com, www.bobartsinstitute.edu), located in Greenwood on a hill above the highway marked by waving Rasta-colored flags, is a bold project dreamed up by Ras Astor Black to draw Jamaica's youth into a technologically focused education in the arts, with music and production courses. As an annex to the school, the vision includes a **Reggae Walk of Fame,** where artists deemed

Wagon wheels and a variety of other colonial-era knick-knacks decorate the courtyard veranda of Greenwood Great House.

honorable will be inducted once per month. Black lives up on a hill between Falmouth and Greenwood, where he has created the Reggae Village. He intends to host regular live concerts to appeal to the masses of tourists who arrive expecting to see more in the way of live reggae music, like they are accustomed to seeing in the United States and Europe.

Plantation Tours

Several plantations in the area offer visitors a chance to learn about Jamaica's principal agricultural products—from those that were important historically to crops adapted to the modern economy. These include Croydon, John's Hall, and Mountain Valley Rafting, which offers a basic banana plantation tour.

Croydon Plantation (contact Tony Henry, tel. 876/979-8267, tlhenry20@hotmail.com, www.croydonplantation.com, open Tues., Thurs., and Fri., as well as other days when cruise ships are in port) is a pineapple and coffee plantation located at the base of the Catadupa Mountains and was the birthplace

of slave rebellion leader and national hero Sam Sharpe. The walking tour takes visitors through a working section of the plantation with an accompanying narrative, with three refreshment stops allowing visitors to sample some of the 12 different kinds of pineapple grown on the estate, in addition to other crops like jackfruit, sugarcane, and Otaheite apple, depending on what's in season. The tour includes a typical Jamaican country lunch. Total tour time from pickup to return is six hours, and the cost (US$65 per person) includes transportation, refreshments, and lunch. Croydon Plantation has the only privately owned forest reserve in the country. The 53-hectare estate is owned by Dalkeith Hanna, with Tony Henry, a partner in the tour operation.

John's Hall Adventure Tour (tel. 876/971-7776, relax.resort@cwjamaica.com, www.johnshalladventuretour.com) offers a plantation tour (US$70 per person inclusive of jerk lunch and fruits) with a historical and contextual commentary by the guides. Stops along the way include the Parish Church, Sam

Sharpe Square, and Mt. Olive Basic School. John's Hall Adventure Tour also operates the **Jamaica Rhythm Tour** (6–9 P.M. Wed. and Sun., US$80 inclusive of dinner), a musical show held at John's Hall featuring old-time heritage (from Maypole dancing and limbo to mento). Both tours include transportation from Mobay area hotels.

BEACHES

Walter Fletcher Beach is the location of **Aquasol Theme Park,** where go-carts, bumper boats, water sports, and two tennis courts heighten the entertainment inherent in the small strip of sand facing Mobay's harbor. The beach is located on the Hip Strip across from The Pork Pit.

Cornwall Beach (US$5, 8 A.M.–6 P.M. daily, tel. 876/979-0102) is wedged between the beaches for what was Breezes Montego Bay and DeCameron. The beach is owned by the St. James Parish Council and managed by David Chung. It was renovated in 2009 with clean restrooms, changing rooms, and showers, and there's a restaurant and beach bar. "Irie Mon" beach parties including a lunch buffet and open bar (US$80/person), with live music and entertainment are held on Wednesdays 11:30 A.M.–3:30 P.M. when a Carnival cruise ship delivers partygoers.

Tropical Beach is a decent, narrow strip of sand on the far side of the airport with the best windsurfing and Jet Ski rental outfit in Mobay. The beach isn't a bad spot for a dip, but it's not a destination for spending the whole day unless you're there for the water sports. To get to Tropical Beach turn left after the airport, heading east toward Ironshore and Rose Hall.

Sunset Beach (10 A.M.–6 P.M., US$60 adult, US$40 children for all-inclusive day pass) is the private beach for Sunset Beach Resort (tel. 876/979-8800 or U.S. tel 800/234-1707, www.sunsetbeachresort.com), which occupies the tip of the peninsula known as Freeport. The resort has a small water park with large pools and slides, as well as excellent tennis facilities. The day pass includes food and drink at the main buffet-style restaurant and several bars scattered throughout the property. To get to Sunset Beach continue past the cruise ship terminal on Southern Cross Boulevard.

Dead End Beach is the best free public beach in close proximity to the Hip Strip at the heart of Mobay's tourism scene. Sandals Carlyle faces the beach, which borders the end of the runway at Donald Sangster International Airport. The beach is located on Kent Avenue, better known as Dead End Road.

One Man Beach and **Dump-Up Beach,** located across from KFC and Mobay's central roundabout, are venues for occasional events and horse grazing. The beach here is no good for swimming however, as the city's effluent emerges from a neighboring gulley.

Old Steamer Beach is located 100 yards past the Shell gas station heading west out of Hopewell, Hanover. An embankment leads down to the skeleton of the U.S.S. *Caribou,* a steamer dating from 1887 that washed off its mooring from Mobay. You can hang your towel on the skeleton ship and take a swim at one of the nicest beaches around, which only gets busy on weekends when locals come down in droves to stir the crystal clear waters.

◀ Doctors Cave Beach

Doctors Cave Beach (US$5) is the see-and-be-seen Hip Strip beach that is always happening. The beach is a favorite for the area's uptown youth on weekends, and a popular venue for full moon parties and other events and activities. The Groovy Grouper, situated to one side of the beach near the entrance, is a dependable spot for seafood and continental fare.

ENTERTAINMENT AND EVENTS
Bars and Clubs

For an early evening drink, the **Montego Bay Yacht Club** (10 A.M.–10 P.M. daily) is a popular spot among the uptown crowd, especially on Fridays. The **HouseBoat Bar** is also a popular early evening spot, while **Mobay Proper** (44 Fort St., tel. 876/940-1233, noon–2 A.M. daily) has the most consistently happening local scene every night of the week.

Hilites Cafe, Bar and Gift Shop (19 Queens Dr., tel. 876/979-9157, jamaica_flamingo_ltd@hotmail.com, 8:30 A.M.–6 P.M. daily) has a great view over the harbor and airport and is another great spot for an early evening drink or to watch the planes take off and land from Sangster Airport.

Margaritaville (Gloucester Ave., tel. 876/952-4777, 11 A.M.–you say when daily, US$10) is a wildly popular restaurant and bar with a water slide dropping off into the sea and giant trampoline inner tubes just offshore for use by customers. The restaurant serves dishes like cheeseburgers, jerk chicken and pork, and lobster (US$9–28), while almost every night of the week has a different theme: Tuesday is Caribbean night, which shifts each week to a different cultural theme—Latin, soca, etc.; Wild Wednesdays features wet T-shirt contests and Jell-O wrestling; Thursday is ladies' night, where women enter free till midnight; on Fridays there is a rotating guest selector or featured artist; and Saturday is World Beat Night with a sound system.

Margaritaville is the brainchild of a Jamaican partnership between Ian Dear and Brian Jardim, who struck a deal with Jimmy Buffet to carry his franchise in the Caribbean. In 10 years the pair has grown a business venture that is today a fixture in the three major tourism hubs: Ocho Rios, Negril, and Mobay, now with a branch at Sangster Airport as well.

Blue Beat (Gloucester Ave., tel. 876/952-4777, 6 P.M.–2 A.M. daily, free entry) is Margaritaville's more sophisticated and upscale cousin, located at the same property under the same ownership. The laid-back club features a resident DJ every night and live jazz Wednesday, Thursday, and Sunday 10 P.M.–2 A.M.

Jamaican Bobsled Cafe (69 Gloucester Ave., tel. 876/940-7009) is a popular bar serving bar food and pizza, and it offers delivery. The bar is at the center of the action on the Hip Strip.

Royal Stocks (Half Moon Shopping Village, tel. 876/953-9770) is an English pub–style bar and restaurant, serving pricey international cuisine. The air-conditioned bar is a great place to go when missing the cool of England, though the beer selection is not the same as back home: Guinness, Red Stripe, and Heineken are the only brews on offer.

The Keg (across from the fire station, no phone) is a local dive bar and a good place to soak up the local scene and listen to oldies.

Billiards

Mobay Proper (44 Fort St., tel. 876/940-1233, noon–2 A.M. daily) is the best place to grab a beer (US$2) and play some billiards (US$1 per game).

Rehab Pool Bar & Lounge (contact proprietor Gary Rose, cell tel. 876/409-1130, 6 P.M.–2 A.M. daily), located across from Lover's Park, next door to China House Restaurant, offers billiards (US$5/45 minutes or US$1 per game in the more spacious room with a/c at seven tables; this place opened in February 2009.

Live Music

Unfortunately, live music in Mobay is hard to come by—in sharp contrast to decades past when there was an active regular music scene. Today, the all-inclusive resorts have house bands that entertain the hotel guests, who are often discouraged from leaving the compound. Nevertheless, there is often live jazz at Day-O Plantation, as well as at Blue Beat, and Margaritaville. Of course if you want world-class music the best time to visit is during Reggae Sumfest (July) or the Jazz and Blues Festival (January). Catherine Hall Entertainment Center, the main venue for Sumfest, also holds occasional stage show concerts throughout the year.

Festivals and Events

Several annual festivals draw thousands from around the island and abroad, chief among them being **Jamaica Jazz and Blues** (www.airjamaicajazzandblues.com) and **Reggae**

Sumfest (www.reggaesumfest.com). The Montego Bay Yacht Club (tel. 876/979-8038, fax 876/979-8262, mbyc@cwjamaica.com, www.mobayyachtclub.com) has its share of events, including annual and biannual yacht races and a **Marlin Festival.** In Albert Town, Trelawny, the highlight of the year is the **Yam Festival** (www.stea.net/yam.htm), which is a family fun day centered on one of the island's most important staple foods, with tugs of war, beauty competitions, and, of course, music. Jamaica's **Carnival** season also brings at least one night of events to Mobay, with a free concert at Dump-Up Beach.

In the hills above Mobay, the Rastafarian community of Pitfour hosts annual **Nyabinghi sessions,** lasting for days to commemorate the coronation of the late Ethiopian Emperor Haile Selassie I, as well as to commemorate the Coral Gardens Massacre on Good Friday. Sadly, the area has fallen into disrepute over the last few years due to crime and violence. Visitors to Pitfour should proceed with caution.

Art and Theater
Alpha Arts (tel. 876/979-3479, cell tel. 876/605-9130, alphaarts@hotmail.com, www.alphaarts.com), adjacent to Sahara de la Mar resort in Reading, produces and sells on-site a variety of colorful ceramics.

Fairfield Theatre (Fairfield Rd., tel. 876/952-0182, US$10) is the only venue in the Mobay area for small, amateur theatrical productions that strive to uphold professional standards. Performances are generally held on weekends. Fairfield Theatre was originally founded as Montego Bay Little Theatre Movement in 1975 by Paul Methuen and Henry and Greta Fowler. The theatrical company was named after the Little Theatre Movement in Kingston, which was formed by Jamaican cultural icons like Louise Bennett. Contact theater chairman Douglas Prout (cell tel. 876/909-9364, dprout@globeins.com, d_freezing@hotmail.com) for more information or call the theater directly for performance schedules.

Mostly contemporary works from the best Jamaican and Caribbean writers are performed at the Fairfield Theatre, but the company produces works from a wide range of playwrights from Shakespeare to Noel Coward, Peter Schaeffer, Lorraine Hansbury, and Neil Simon. Caribbean writers such as Derek Walcott, Errol Hill, and Douglas Archibald have been produced to critical acclaim, but greater audience appeal has been found with the current crop of Jamaican playwrights that include Basil Dawkins, Trevor Rhone, Patrick Brown, and David Heron.

Palace Multiplex (Eldemire Dr., next to Jerky's, tel. 876/971-5550, movie times tel. 876/979-8624) is a cinema showing standard Hollywood films.

SHOPPING
Montego Bay is full of duty-free stores and gift shops.

Klass Traders (Fort St., tel. 876/952-5782) produces attractive handmade leather sandals from a workshop adjacent to Mobay Proper. Leroy Thompson (cell tel. 876/546-8657) is the head craftsman.

Rastafari Art (42 Hart St., tel. 876/885-7674 or 876/771-7533) has a variety of red, gold, and green items, including flags, belts, T-shirts, bags, and friendship bands that make inexpensive, authentic, and lightweight gifts and souvenirs.

For clothes, try **Lloyd's** (26 St. James St., tel. 876/952-3172), which has a great selection of trendy urban and roots wear and carries the CY Evolution brand.

Craft centers abound in Mobay, from Harbour Street to Kent Avenue to Charles Gordon Market and Montego Bay Craft Market. A discriminating eye is required at all these markets to sift out the junk from quality Jamaica-produced crafts.

Freeport Cruise Ship Terminal has several shops, most of which carry overpriced souvenirs and mass-produced crafts items of little inherent value.

Duty-free shops are found anywhere you glance in Mobay, concentrated around City Centre Complex, the Hip Strip, and at the Half Moon Shopping Village east of town. The new Rose Hall Shopping Complex also has its share of duty-free items.

Bookland (34 Union St., 876/940-6185, bookland-mobay@cwjamaica.com, Mon.–Fri. 9 A.M.–6 P.M., Sat. 10 A.M.–5 P.M.) has the best selection of Caribbean books, as well as local and international magazines.

Sangster's Bookstore is at 2 St. James Street (tel. 876/952-0319).

Habanos Gift Shop (Shop #1, Casa Blanca Building, Gloucester Ave., tel. 876/940-4139, cell tel. 876/884-8656, habanoscigars1492@ yahoo.com), run by Raj Jeswani, sells Cuban and Jamaican cigars out of a walk-in humidor, plus rum, spices, coffee, and a full array of "Jamaica no problem mon" T-shirts, trinkets, and souvenirs.

Tad's International Records (retail outlet in the departure lounge at Sangster International Airport) has an extensive catalog of reggae.

Great River Studios (contact Paul Taylor, cell tel. 876/609-6266) is a recording studio operated by the owners of Spyglass Hill and located on the same estate as the villa. The studio rents for US$30–50 per hour with Pro Tools, voicing and live band rooms, and a two-inch analog tape. Led by studio musician, Palma Taylor, it's based just outside Hopewell.

SPORTS AND RECREATION

Tropical Beach Fitness (tel. 876/952-6510, tropicalfitness@hotmail.com, Mon.–Thurs., 6 A.M.–10 P.M., Fri. 6 A.M.–9 P.M., Sat. 9 A.M.–4 P.M., Sun. 9 A.M.–2 P.M.) is a decent beachfront gym with free weights, treadmills, bicycles, stair steppers, and weight benches. Membership is offered by the day (US$5) and month (US$30). The club has about 200 local members, with two trainers available for an extra fee.

Water Sports

The **Montego Bay Yacht Club** (tel. 876/979-8038, fax 876/979-8262, mbyc@cwjamaica. com, www.mobayyachtclub.com) was refurbished in 2006 with a new building, landscaped grounds, and a small swimming pool. The club is a warm and friendly family environment with

a great bar and restaurant, making it the place in western Jamaica for sailing, fishing, or just to hang out and make friends. Entertainment at the club is facilitated by pool tables, foosball, and table tennis. Every Friday, the club hosts a buffet dinner. Social and sailing membership is available by the day (US$5) or by the year (US$150). The annual fee grants members access to the Royal Jamaica Yacht Club in Kingston as well.

The Mobay Yacht Club is the final destination of the famous **Pineapple Cup Race** (www.montegobayrace.com), which covers 1,305 kilometers of water from its starting point in Fort Lauderdale. This classic race—a beat, a reach, and a run—is held in February of every odd year. Other events include the annual J-22 International Regatta held every December, and the Great Yacht Race, which precedes every Easter Regatta, a fun-filled, friendly, and competitive multi-class regatta. The International Marlin Fishing Tournament is held every fall. Sailing camps for children are held during the summer and courses offered to adults based on demand.

If you arrive in Jamaica on a private vessel, the Mobay Yacht Club has some of the lowest docking fees anywhere (US$0.87 per foot 1–7 days), which are reduced even further for longer stays (US$0.50 per foot for 8–30 days). Utilities are metered and charged accordingly, while boats at anchor can use the club facilities for the regular daily membership fee (US$5 per person). Mobay's mangrove areas in the Bogue Lagoon are often used as a hurricane hole for small vessels. All charges carry 16.50 percent tax.

Aquasol Theme Park (Gloucester Ave., tel. 876/979-9447 or 876/940-1344, 9 A.M.–6 P.M. Mon.–Thurs., till 10 P.M. Fri.–Sun., US$5 adults, US$3 children under 12) is a small theme park located on Walter Fletcher Beach, with go carts (US$3 single-seated, US$7 double), two tennis courts (operated by Steve Nolan, cell tel. 876/364-9293, 6:30 A.M.–10 P.M. daily, US$6/hr.), billiard tables (US$.50 per game), a video games room, glass-bottomed boat excursions to the coral reef (US$25 per person for a 30-min. tour), and personal watercraft like Jet Skis ($75 for 30 min.). There's also a sports bar with satellite TV and the Voyage restaurant (US$5–10), serving fried chicken, fried fish, and jerk. A gym on property, Mighty Moves (tel. 876/952-8608, 7 A.M.–8 P.M. daily, US$8), has free weights, weight machines, and aerobics classes included with the day pass.

Tropical Beach Water Sports (tel. 876/940-0836, 9 A.M.–5 P.M. daily) is run by Chaka Brown with professional-quality equipment, including windsurfing sailboards (US$45/hour) and Jet Skis (US$75/half-hour, US$130/hour). Bogue Lagoon excursions are also offered (US$220/hour for up to six people).

Ezee Fishing (Denise Taylor, cell tel. 876/381-3229 or 876/995-2912, chokey@reggaefemi.com, dptgonefishing@hotmail.com, www.montego-bay-jamaica.com/ajal/noproblem, US$450 half day, US$890 full day) operates a 39-foot Phoenix Sport Fisher for deep-sea expeditions, offering a good chance of catching big game like wahoo, blue marlin, or dorado (depending on time of year). Ezee also offers sailing charters (www.jamaicawatersports.com) on catamaran Suncat and trimaran Freestyle vessels (US$400 for two-hour sails for up to 10 people).

Rapsody Tours, Cruises & Charters operates the **Dreamer Catamaran Cruises** (contact Donna Lee, tel. 876/979-0102, reservations@dreamercatamarans.com, 10 A.M.–1 P.M. and 3 P.M.–6 P.M. Mon.–Sat., US$65 per person, reservations required) with two daily three-hour cruises on its two 53-foot catamarans and one 65-foot catamaran. The catamarans depart from Cornwall Beach for morning and afternoon cruises at 10 A.M. and 3 P.M., and an evening cruise on Thursdays and Saturdays leaves from Doctors Cave Beach a 5 P.M. The excursion includes an open bar and use of snorkeling gear.

Two-hour **Calico Sunset Cruises** (5–7 P.M. Tues.–Sun., US$40 adults, US$20 children 3–11) are offered on the same Calico sailboat, with an optional dinner package (US$65) that includes a four-course meal at the Town House Restaurant following the sail.

Lark Cruises by Barrett Adventures (contact Captain Carolyn Barrett, Barrett Adventures, cell tel. 876/382-6384, info@barrettadventures.com, www.barrettadventures.

com) operates half-day (US$400) and full-day (US$600) cruises out of Mobay for up to three passengers, with snorkeling and a Jamaican lunch included (US$100 for each additional person up to 10). Weekly charters are also offered (US$3,000 for up to six, plus provisions), inclusive of captain and cook. Charter cruise options include excursions to Negril, Port Antonio, or even Cuba, contingent upon favorable weather conditions.

Golf

Montego Bay is the best base for golfing in Jamaica, with the highest concentration of courses on a nice variety of terrains, some with gorgeous rolling hills, others seaside, all within the immediate vicinity.

White Witch Golf Course (Rose Hall, tel. 876/953-2800 or 876/518-0174, www.rose-hall.com, 6:30 A.M.–9 P.M. daily) is the most spectacular course in Jamaica, for its views and rolling greens. The course has a special for Ritz guests (US$180 per person includes greens fees, cart, and caddy, not including US$20 recommended gratuity per player). The course is also open to nonguests (US$200 includes cart caddy and 18 holes, but not gratuity). White Witch offers a Twilight Golf Special (US$99 per person, inclusive of cart, caddy, and greens fee, after 2:30 P.M.). The last tee time is at 4:30 P.M.

A gorgeous clubhouse features beautiful views and the **White Witch Restaurant** (noon–9 P.M.), open to nongolfers as well, and a pro shop. The restaurant serves sandwiches, soups, and salads for lunch and fish and steak for dinner.

Cinnamon Hill Golf Course (Rose Hall, tel. 876/953-2650) is operated by Rose Hall Resort and offers special rates to in-house guests (US$141, inclusive of cart, caddy, and greens fees—extended to Half Moon and Sandals guests). The club also offers a Twilight Special (US$99 after 1:30 P.M.), in addition to the standard rack rate (US$160 inclusive of cart, caddy, and greens fees) with club rental an additional charge (US$40–50). Recommended caddy tip is US$10–15 per player. Cinnamon Hill is the only course in Jamaica that's on the coast. Holes five and six are directly at the water's edge. There is a gorgeous waterfall at the foot of Cinnamon Hill great house, which was owned by Johnny Cash until his death.

Half Moon Golf Course (Rose Hall, tel. 876/953-2560, www.halfmoongolf.com) is a Robert Trent Jones Jr.–designed course, with reduced rates for Half Moon Guests (US$75 for nine holes, US$105 for 18 holes). Rates for nonguests are US$90/150 for 9/18 holes, US$12/20 for caddy, US$40/50 for club rental, and US$25/35 for cart. Half Moon is a walkable course.

SuperClubs Golf Course at Iron Shore (tel. 876/953-3682) is a very respectable 18-hole course, with regular greens fees (US$50) waived for SuperClubs hotel guests. Caddy (US$11/16 for 9/18 holes) and cart (US$17/35 for 9/18 holes) fees are the lowest in Mobay; many prefer the course, in spite of it never having hosted a PGA tournament. Shelly Clifford is the friendly golf course manager.

Horseback Riding

Half Moon Equestrian Centre (Half Moon Resort, tel. 876/953-2286, r.delisser@cw-jamaica.com, www.horsebackridingjamaica.com) has the most impressive stables open to the public in Jamaica, for beginning to experienced riders. The center offers a pony ride for children under 6 for US$20 and a 40-minute beginner ride for US$60 (suitable for children over 6), a beach ride for US$80 that includes a horseback swim (for riders over age 8), and 30-minute private lessons for any experience level that can include basic dressage, jumping, and polo.

Chukka Caribbean (www.chukkacaribbean.com) offers a Ride 'N Swim tour in Sandy Bay, Hanover, about a half-hour drive west of Mobay.

ACCOMMODATIONS

Accommodation options vary widely from cheap dives and inexpensive guesthouses to luxury villas and world-class hotels. In the center of town, on Queens Drive (Top Road), and to the west in Reading there are several low-cost options, while the mid-range hotels are concentrated around the Hip Strip along Gloucester Avenue (Bottom Road) and just east of the airport. Rose Hall is the area's most glamorous address, both for its private villas and mansions surrounding the White Witch Golf Course, and for the Ritz-Carlton and neighboring Half Moon, the most exclusive resorts in town. Also on the eastern side of town is Sandals Royal Caribbean, easily the chain's most luxurious property, complete with a private island.

Along the Hip Strip several mid-range hotels provide direct access to Mobay's nightlife, a mix of bars and a few clubs, and guesthouses farther afield offer great rates.

Mobay is the principal entry point for most tourists arriving on the island, many of whom stay at one of the multitude of hotels in the immediate vicinity. The old Ironshore and Rose Hall estates east along the coast are covered in luxury and mid-range hotels.

Under US$100

☑ Altamont West (tel. 876/620-4540, www.altamontwesthotel.com, altamontwesthotel@yahoo.com, US$90 d) is the latest boutique hotel to crop up along the Hip Strip in Montego Bay. The Altamont West marks the first foray into Western Jamaica for the Jarrett family, which has run the Altamont Court hotel in Kingston for years. Rooms at the Altamont West are cozy and well appointed, with flat panel TVs, Internet, air-conditioning, and private baths with hot water. Linens are soft and clean. The hotel is ideally situated across from Walter Fletcher Beach, a short walk to bars and restaurants along Gloucestershire Avenue, as well as Doctor's Cave and Cornwall beaches.

Palm Bay Guest House (Reading Rd., Bogue, tel. 876/952-2274) has decent, basic rooms (US$48) with air-conditioning and hot water in private bathrooms. While not the most glamorous location in town, opposite Mobay's biggest government housing project—Bogue Village, built to formalize the squatters of Canterbury—Palm Bay is quiet and safe and appreciably well removed from the hustle and bustle along the Hip Strip.

Big Apple Rooms (18 Queens Dr., tel. 876/952-7240, bigapplehotel1@yahoo.com, www.bigapplejamaica.com, US$65) is a no-frills hotel perched on the hill above the airport. The basic rooms have private baths with hot water, air-conditioning, and cable TV. There is a pool deck with a view of the ocean.

Satori Resort & Spa (tel. 876/952-6133, www.satorijamaica.com, US$65/85 low/high season) has 21 basic, no-frills, waterfront rooms with air-conditioning, cable TV, and hot water in private bathrooms. The hotel faces Mobay's lagoon from its location west of town in Reading.

Sahara de la Mar (Reading, tel. 876/952-2366, sahara.hotels@yahoo.com, www.saharahotels.com, US$60) is a 24-room oceanfront property nicely designed to hug the coast and provide a central protected swimming area. Amenities include hot water in private bathrooms, fans, air-conditioning, and TV. Food is prepared to order in the restaurant on the ground level.

Calabash Resorts (5 Queens Dr., tel. 876/952-3900 or 876/952-3999, www.calabashresorts.com, US$77–87 low season, US$105–115 high season) has a variety of basic rooms and studios with air-conditioning and hot water in en suite bathrooms. Some rooms command a view of the bay, and the pool has a great view over the city and bay.

K Hartley House (contact Sandra Kennedy, tel. 876/956-7101, cell tel. 876/371-3693, sandravkennedy@yahoo.com, US$50/ night per person including breakfast) is a lovely B&B located on a two-acre property at Tamarind Hill by the Great River, on the border of Hanover and St. James about 20 minutes from Sangster International Airport. Four rooms in the villa are rented, with the innkeepers living on property. Rooms are appointed in traditional colonial style with four-poster queen-size beds, or two twins in one room, and have sitting areas, ceiling fans and private baths. The stone-cut villa

was designed by architect Robert Hartley as a satellite property to Round Hill in 1965. Guests have access to a common area with a library and TV room. Meals can be prepared to order (US$8–12). Wi-Fi, tea, and coffee are complimentary all day long. Guests have a choice of low-calorie, continental, Jamaican, or English breakfast.

Villa Nia (cell tel. 876/382-6384, info@barrettadventures.com, www.carolynscaribbeancottages.com/VillaNia/indexnia.htm, US$85–95 per room) is a four-bedroom duplex property owned by Ron Hagler, located right on the water adjacent to Sandals Montego Bay on the opposite side of the airport from the Hip Strip. The rooms rent independently and feature either queen-size or king-size beds with sitting areas, small kitchens, and balconies. Each room has a private bath with hot water.

US$100-250

K Richmond Hill (tel. 876/952-3859, info@richmond-hill-inn.com, www.richmond-hill-inn.com, US$70/115 low/high season) is located at the highest point in the vicinity of downtown Mobay, with what is easily the best view in town from a large terraced swimming pool area and open-air dining room. While the accommodations fall short of luxurious, the sheets are clean, the restaurant is excellent, and the pool area's unmatched view and free wireless Internet access make Richmond Hill one of the best values in town.

Gloustershire Hotel (Gloucester Ave., tel. 876/952-4420 or U.S. tel. 877/574-8497, res@gloustershire.com, www.gloustershire.com, US$100/120 low/high season) is well situated across from Doctor's Cave Beach on the Hip Strip. It has a total of 88 rooms, many with balconies with a view of the bay. Other amenities include 27-inch TVs, hot water, and air-conditioning.

El Greco Resort (Queens Dr., tel. 876/940-6116 or U.S. tel. 888/354-7326, elgreco4@cwjamaica.com, www.elgrecojamaica.com, US$125/134 low/high season) is a large complex of suites overlooking the bay with a long stairway down to Doctors Cave Beach across Gloucester Avenue. Suites feature living areas with ceiling fans, air-conditioning in the bedrooms, and private baths with hot water. Many of the suites have balconies with sea views.

At the **Wexford Hotel** (39 Gloucester Ave., tel. 876/952-2854, wexford@cwjamaica.com, www.thewexfordhotel.com, US$144/177 low/high season), most rooms have two double beds, all with private baths and full amenities. Two rooms have king-size beds that can be requested. The hotel has a restaurant, The Rosella restaurant (7 A.M.–11 P.M. daily) that does an excellent Sunday Jamaican brunch buffet (US$10), well attended by locals and tourists alike.

Casa Blanca Beach Hotel (Gloucester Ave., tel. 876/952-0720, info@casablanca-jamaica.com, www.casablancajamaica.com, US$148, cash only) was, in its heyday, one of Mobay's most glamorous hotels. Only around 20 of the hotel's 72-rooms have been in operation over the past years, however, with a construction effort brought under way more recently. The rooms all overlook the water along the prime strip of Gloucester Avenue adjacent to Doctors Cave Beach. Unfortunately, poor maintenance and signs of neglect abound. Nonetheless the hotel sits on the best location in town for bars and nightlife. Norman Pushell is owner/manager. Amenities include private bath with hot water, air-conditioning, waterfront balconies, and cable TV. Guests get free entry to Doctors Cave Beach.

Doctors Cave Beach Hotel (Gloucester Ave., tel. 876/952-4355, info@doctorscave.com, www.doctorscave.com, from US$140/190 low/high season) is a no-frills hotel catering to those looking for direct, easy access to Doctors Cave Bathing Club across the street. Amenities include cable TV, air-conditioning, and hot water. Rooms are spacious with either a garden or poolside view. The cozy den-like bar has a Rum Punch Party happy hour with free rum punch 6–7 P.M. Tuesday and Saturday, and two-for-one rum punch thereafter.

Over US$250

Coyaba Beach Resort (Rose Hall, tel. 876/953-9150, www.coyabaresortjamaica.com, US$240/320 low/high season) is one of the most professionally run hotels in Mobay, with impeccably clean and well-appointed rooms with all the amenities of home and pleasantly unobtrusive decor. The hotel grounds are also attractive, with a pool and private beach area. The only drawback to the property is its proximity to the airport and occasional roar of a departing flight. On the other hand, the proximity is also an advantage for the majority of guests, who tend to be weekend getaway visitors to Jamaica who stay three or four nights on average. Coyaba is located 10 minutes east of the airport and 15 minutes from Mobay's Hip Strip.

Ritz-Carlton Rose Hall (Rose Hall, tel. 876/953-2800 or U.S. tel. 800/241-3333, rc.mbjrz.concierge@ritzcarlton.com, www.ritzcarlton.com, US$189/499 low/high season room-only, US$429/899 low/high season all-inclusive) is a 427-room, AAA Five-Diamond golf and spa resort with the Rose Hall Estate Great House as its historical centerpiece. Rose Hall is easily one of the nicest Ritz properties in the world, with a private beach and two world-class golf courses right next door. A 1,003-square-meter ballroom and meeting space for up to 700 people make the Ritz one of the most popular corporate retreat destinations in the Caribbean, with on-site spa facilities and Jamaican touches to help ease any work-related tension. The property also boasts a state-of-the-art fitness center. The rooms at the Ritz uphold the highest standards of the brand, with attractive art depicting Jamaican flora and fauna throughout.

Half Moon Resort (Rose Hall, tel. 876/953-2211, reservations@halfmoonclub.com, www.halfmoon.com, US$250–400 low season, US$1250–1,800 high season) is one of the most upscale resorts in Jamaica, comprising an assortment of rooms, cottages, and villas. Most of the cottages and all the villas have private pools. Set on a 400-acre estate, the resort has 33 staffed villas with 3–7 bedrooms, 152 suites,

MONTEGO BAY

© OLIVER HILL

Fern Tree Spa at Half Moon Resort sets a high bar for luxurious pampering.

and 46 rooms. The cottages are tastefully furnished and cozier than the villas, which can feel cavernous due to their immense size and vary considerably in decor based on the taste of their individual owners.

Half Moon attracts golfers to its championship, par-72 Robert Trent Jones Sr. course; it is also a favorite for tennis players with 13 lighted courts. A range of water sports are on offer, and Half Moon is the only resort in Jamaica to have its own dolphin lagoon, operated by Dolphin Cove exclusively for Half Moon guests. Food at the estate's six restaurants is top-notch, with a number of snack bars dotting the property for quick bites. Also on the resort is the recently renovated **Fern Tree Spa,** among the best in the Caribbean, and a shopping complex. The crescent-shaped Half Moon Beach is one of the finest private beaches in the Mobay area.

All-Inclusive Resorts

Sunset Beach (tel. 876/979-8800, US tel. 800/234-1707, reservations@sunset-mobay.com, www.sunsetbeachresort.com, US$280/320 low/high season) occupies the choice property on the Freeport peninsula, which is also home to the Yacht Club and the cruise ship terminal. Sunset Beach is a 430-room mass-tourism venture and part of the Sunset Resorts group. It is very comparable to the group's property in Ocho Rios in catering to everyone with its motto, "Always for Everyone, Uniquely Jamaican," but especially popular among families on a budget. The rooms are divided between a main building and smaller structures on the other side of a large pool area. Rooms either face out to sea or toward downtown Montego Bay. The hotel has excellent tennis facilities, a popular water park with slides, a great beach, and spa facilities. Food is mass-market American fare with large buffet spreads at Banana Walk, complemented by Italian Botticelli, and pan-Asian Silk Road. Several bars dot the property offering unlimited bottom-shelf product. This is a convenient place to stay for Reggae Sumfest, with a hotel shuttle to the Catherine Hall Entertainment Center a few minutes away. It is not centrally located for walking the Hip Strip, but still within 10 minutes by cab.

Royal DeCameron Montego Beach (2 Gloucester Ave., tel. 876/952-4340 or 876/952-4346, ventas.jam@decameron. com, www.decameron.com, US$116/240 per person low/high season) is a budget-minded all-inclusive recently opened as the chain's second property in Jamaica. At times it can be hard to get through for a reservation, but otherwise the property could be a good value when compared to the other all-inclusive prices.

Holiday Inn Sunspree (Rose Hall, tel. 876/953-2485, www.montegobayjam.sunspreeresorts.com, US$315/535 low/high season) has the most decidedly mass-market ambience of all the all-inclusive resorts.

Secrets St. James and **Secrets Wild Orchid** (tel. 876/953-6600, reservations. sesmb@secretsresorts.com, www.secretsresorts.com, US$188/326 low/high), located next to one another on the southwestern tip of the Freeport peninsula, opened in March 2010. All 700 suites at the two properties have essentially the same layout, with whirlpool tubs and either a balcony or patio. The food is above average for all-inclusive hotels, with an excellent breakfast buffet spread and fine dining restaurants specializing in French, Italian, and Japanese cuisine.

Sandals Carlyle Montego Bay (Kent Ave., a.k.a. Dead End Rd., tel. 876/952-4141 or 888/sandals (888/726-3257), chbrown@grp. sandals.com, www.sandals.com, starting at US$334 d all-inclusive), formerly Sandals Inn, is a 52-room property that has been undergoing a transformation over the past few years as its renovations move forward little by little. Located along Dead End Road, steps from Mobay's Hip Strip, this is the most proximate Sandals property to the city's buzzing bars and nightlife, with the popular Dead End Beach located across the street. Rooms have balconies looking over the central pool area and out to sea. Tennis and beach volleyball courts are found at the far end of the property. A mix of standard rooms and suites have king-size beds and private baths, all with air-conditioning and cable TV.

Sandals Montego Bay (tel. 800/726-3257, www.sandals.com, US$970–4,050) was the first Sandals property and remains the group's flagship resort. Located near the end of the runway, guests are encouraged to wave to the planes as they fly overhead. The property boasts the largest private beach in Jamaica with 251 rooms, a Red Lane Spa, butler service in the highest suite category, four pools and four whirlpool tubs, private villa cottages, and a private wedding chapel. The resort has a series of gazebos along the beach, as well as canopy beach beds to rent for an additional charge. Sandals imposes a minimum stay of three nights at all its properties. Promotions are ongoing throughout the year, slashing rates by as much as 65 percent.

Sandals Royal Caribbean (Mahoe Bay, Ironshore, tel. 876/953-2231, srjmail@grp. sandals.com, starting at US$473 d with a minimum three-night stay) is the most opulent Sandals hotel in Montego Bay, with 197 rooms and suites well deserving of the

a beach bed at Sandals Montego Bay

© OLIVER HILL

chain's "Luxury Included" motto. The suites are over-the-top with wood paneling, large flat-panel TVs, and tiled baths with standing showers and tubs. Balconies look over the courtyard and out to sea, with steps off ground floor suites leading directly into a large pool. The private island at Sandals Royal Caribbean is the trademark feature, where boats shuttle guests out for dinner or to laze away the days on the fine-sand beach. Gazebos are spaced across the property at the end of piers, favorite locations for wedding vows.

Riu Montego Bay (tel. 876/940-8010, www.riu.com, US$115/160) is a 680-room all-inclusive resort with standard double and suite rooms and an immense swimming pool. Suites have hydro-massage tubs and lounge areas. All rooms have a mini-bar, satellite TV, air-conditioning, balconies, and en suite baths. The resort offers a host of activities, including water sports and tennis on two hard-surface courts. The gym has a weight room, sauna, and Jacuzzi. The resort is located in Ironshore, near the end of the runway for Donald Sangster International Airport, next door to Sandals Royal Caribbean.

◖ Rose Hall Resort & Spa (Rose Hall, tel. 876/953-2650 or U.S. toll-free 866/799-3661, rosehallroomscontrol@luxuryresorts.com, www.rosehallresort.com, starting at US$149–199 d low season, US$169–219 d high season for room only, US$289–339 d low season, US$309–359 all-inclusive high season), a Hilton Resort, is a 489-room, seven-floor property built in 1974. The hotel underwent a US$40 million renovation in 2008 after being bought by Hilton and boasts a sleek South Beach design. Food is excellent, with indoor and outdoor seating in buffet and à la carte formats, and a seaside bar and grill by the Olympic-size pool directly in front of the hotel. The Sugar Mill Falls Water Park on property boasts a 280-foot water slide for a thrilling ride on tubes, spilling into a freeform pool with a swim-up bar, lazy river, waterfalls, and hot tubs

in a lush garden setting. The beach, located below the main pool and grill area, has fine white sand along a respectable stretch of coast.

Iberostar (tel. 876/680-0000, or US tel. 305/774-9225, reservations@iberostar-hotel.com, www.iberostar.com) completed a massive resort complex in 2007, with three all-inclusive hotels representing three distinct price categories. Guests staying at the more expensive hotels can use the restaurants and facilities of the lower categories, but guests of the lower-category hotels are not permitted on the more expensive properties. The quality of the food varies considerably by the price point, as you'd expect.

The **Iberostar Rose Hall Beach** (starting at US$190/309 per person low/high season) is a 424-room property that caters to the lower end of the Iberostar spectrum. Standard rooms have either one or two beds, and overlook the gardens with junior suites having either ocean view or garden view rooms.

Iberostar Rose Hall Suites (starting at US$235/363 per person low/high season) has 319 rooms, two pools with swim-up bars, and a lazy river meandering across the lawn. All rooms have a suite format with living rooms and mini-bars, with full tubs in the bathrooms of the higher category rooms and either ocean or garden view.

Iberostar Grand Rose Hall (starting at US$336/472 per person low/high season) has 295 rooms, all with living areas, day beds, verandas, bathtubs, and mini-bars. The property has two pools, each with a swim-up bar. The food at Iberostar Grand is excellent and has buffet and à la carte options with top-of-the-line dishes like lobster and steaks.

Villas

Hammerstein Highland House (up Long Hill from Reading in Content, U.S. tel. 805/258-2767, keressapage@yahoo.com, www.highlandhousejamaica.com, US$7,500/9,500 low/high season with four-night minimum for entire property) is a stunning six-bedroom villa on a lush 17-acre property overlooking Montego Bay in the community of Content. Smaller groups can opt to rent a minimum of four bedrooms (US$6,500/8,500 low/high season). There are two king-size beds, one queen-size bed, two rooms with two twin beds, and the last room has a double bed. The two twin rooms can be converted to king-size beds. Amenities include complimentary Wi-Fi, a large pool, and beach club membership at Round Hill. All rooms have air-conditioning and satellite TV. A screened-in yoga pavilion with ceiling fans that accommodates up to 12 adults makes the property a favorite for yoga retreats. The staff includes a housekeeper, butler, cook, laundress, gardener, and farmer. The two-acre organic farm on property supplies much of the food for the villa and is linked with the Anchovy school breakfast program and an orphanage up the road, as part of the villa's support for the One Love Learning Foundation.

Spyglass Hill (contact Paul Taylor tel. 876/601-6456, or cell tel. 876/871-8454, spyglass@cwjamaica.com, www.spyglasshilljamaica.com, 1–4 br US$5,000/5,950; 5–6 br US$7,000/8,950; 7–8 br US$9,300/11,500) is an eight-bedroom, 6,500-square-foot former plantation house set on 10 acres of lush lawns and gardens and named for its breathtaking view over the St. James and Hanover coastline. The property can accommodate up to 18 guests and boasts a 20- by 40-foot pool, as well as a 24-inch wading pool for children. No amenities are left out, with a component stereo system and DVD player in the living room and TVs in all eight bedrooms, seven of which have air-conditioning. DSL Internet and fax are available for guests. The staff includes a cook, butler, housekeepers, laundress, pool maintenance person, gardeners, night watchman, and driver. A gazebo with a stunning oceanview backdrop makes the property a favorite for weddings. Rooms have en suite bathrooms and comfortable furnishings with king-size or queen-size beds, spread across the main house and three outlying buildings located a across the lawn: Tree

House, Garden Room, and the two-bedroom River House, the latter with a 10- by 13-foot plunge pool.

SunVillas (contact Alan Marlor, SunVillas, U.S. tel. 888/625-6007, alan@sunvillas.com, www.sunvillas.com) rents a nice assortment of villas across Jamaica, varying considerably in price while all having much more than the basic amenities. Highlights in the Mobay area include the four-bedroom Afimi property on the Bogue Lagoon in Freeport, the glamorous 10-bedroom Silent Waters villa on the Great River along the St. James–Hanover border, and the six-bedroom Endless Summer and Greatview properties in the auspicious Spring Farm neighborhood, as well as several of the most luxurious villas at Round Hill and Tryall Club.

FOOD
Jamaican
❰ Original Madourie Fast Food (80 Barnett St., contact owner Valtona Madourie, cell tel.

Original Madourie Fast Food is a popular local joint for Jamaican staples.

© OLIVER HILL

876/852-1041, 7 A.M.–midnight Mon.–Sat., US$2.50–4) has been a local favorite for staple Jamaican fare since it was founded in 1976. Specialties include fry chicken, curry goat, oxtail, and brown stew fish. Madourie's is always packed with a clientele that's almost exclusively Jamaican, a testimony to the good food that's reasonably priced.

Musiq (72 Gloucester Ave., 5 P.M.–1 A.M. daily) was opened in July 2009 by Pork Pit owner Uhma Williams as a musically focused bar located next door to her original establishment. The bar features an in-house DJ from Thursday to Sunday playing R&B, hip-hop, reggae, and dancehall. A chic setting with musical motif lends itself to chilling out and watching passersby along the Hip Strip. The bar food is very reasonably priced compared to other establishments along the Strip, with 10 chicken wings going for US$8, a slew of burgers with a variety of seasonings for US$8–12, and soups (US$3) and salads (US$6–9).

Dragon Lounge (Whitehouse, tel. 876/952-1578, 7 A.M.–11 P.M. daily, US$8.50–14), run by Sebil and Peter Tebert, serves excellent seafood dishes, including shrimp, conch, and lobster, in a gritty and rootsy Jamaican bar environment with a dining room out back by the kitchen.

C Adwa Nutrition for Life is the best place in town for natural food. It has three locations, including one full-service, sit-down restaurant (Shops #158–160, City Center, tel. 876/940-7618) and two stores (Shop #7, West F&S Complex, 29–31 Union St., tel. 876/952-2161; and Shop #2, West Gate Plaza, tel. 876/952-6554) with imported and domestic products and delis serving freshly made foods and juice blends. Dishes (US$1–4.50) include curried tofu, peppered veggie steak, and red pea sip, with beverages like cane juice, fruit smoothies, and carrot juice also served.

Ruby Restaurant (Shop #3, Westgate Shopping Centre, tel. 876/952-3199, 8 A.M.–8:30 P.M. Mon.–Sat., US$3.50–11) has Jamaican breakfast dishes like callaloo and codfish, ackee and saltfish, kidney and onion, and brown stew chicken, as well as more international standards like eggs and bacon, French toast, and ham and bacon omelettes. The lunch menu ranges from curry goat to escovitch fish. More expensive dishes include shrimp plates and steamed fish. Sui mein, foo yong, and chow mein are also available.

C Mobay Proper (44 Fort St., tel. 876/940-1233, noon–2 A.M. daily, US$3.50–14) is the in spot for Mobay's party-hearty youth and fashionable businesspeople alike. The food is excellent and a great value, with dishes like fried or jerk chicken, fish done to order, curry goat, roast beef, and steamed, escovitch, or brown stew fish. This is the best place to get a beer (US$2) and play some billiards (US$1 per game).

The Pelican (Gloucester Ave., tel. 876/952-3171, 7 A.M.–11 P.M. daily, US$10–40) serves a mix of local and international dishes at international prices. Jamaican favorites like stewed peas (US$8), curry goat (US$12), steamed or brown stew fish (US$11), and lobster (US$40) complement international staples like cordon bleu (US$17) and hamburgers (US$9).

The **Montego Bay Yacht Club** (Freeport, tel. 876/979-8038, 10 A.M.–10 P.M. daily, US$6–25) has a good menu with burgers, sandwiches, salads, and entrées like lobster and shrimp thermidor, snapper, lamb chops, seafood pasta, coconut curry chicken, and zucchini pasta in a pleasant waterfront setting. A popular buffet dinner (US$14) with a rotating menu is served on Fridays.

Jerk

C Scotchie's (Carol Gardens, tel. 876/953-3301, 11 A.M.–11 P.M. daily, US$4–11) is easily the best jerk in Jamaica, serving pork, chicken, and steamed fish. Sides include breadfruit, festival, and yam. Scotchie's was forced to move back from the expanded highway and took the opportunity to redesign the dining area, adding a nice bar in the open-air courtyard. Scotchie's founder Tony

Rerrie used to have parties where he would bring a master jerk chef from Boston Bay in Portland, where locals claim jerk originated, and patrons would beg him to make the jerk offering a regular thing. He started his first jerk center on the roadside in Montego Bay with a few cinder blocks, some bamboo poles, and a few sheets of zinc roofing.

The Pork Pit (27 Gloucester Ave., tel. 876/940-3008, US$5–11) has jerk by the pound: pork, chicken, ribs, and shrimp.

Jerky's (29 Alice Eldemire Dr., tel. 876/684-9101 or 876/684-9102, 11 A.M.– midnight Sun.–Fri., open later on Sat. for karaoke, US$3–10) has jerk chicken, steamed fish, escovitch fish, ribs, conch, shrimp, and fried fish. There is a large bar where a beer costs US$1.75.

Nyam 'n' Jam (17 Harbour St., tel. 876/952-1922, 7 A.M.–11 P.M. daily, US$3– 4.50) has a variety of Jamaican staples like fried chicken, curry goat, and oxtail. Breakfast items include ackee and saltfish, calaloo and saltfish, brown stew chicken, yam, boiled bananas, and fried dumpling.

Nyam 'n' Jam Jerk Centre (just before descending the hill into Mobay from "top road," a.k.a. Queens Dr., tel. 876/952-1713, 7 A.M.–11 P.M.) has local dishes as well as decent jerk under the same ownership. The jerk center offers delivery in addition to having a small dining area.

Palm Bay Guest House (Bogue Main Rd., 7 A.M.–10 P.M., US$4–6.50) has a small restaurant serving local dishes like curry goat, stew pork, fried chicken, and oxtail, as well as an outdoor jerk center (noon–midnight daily) that serves decent Boston-style jerk.

Pimento's (Reading Rd., cell tel. 876/446-2125, 10 A.M.–7 P.M. Mon.–Sat., US$3–9) is a new jerk and Jamaican food joint just past Bogue in Reading, heading west out of town. Original Jamaican dishes include curry goat, steamed fish, fried chicken, stewed peas with pig tail, fish, and shrimp.

International

Dragon Court (Fairview Shopping Center, Alice Eldemire Dr., Bogue, tel. 876/979-8822 or 876/979-8824, fax 876/979-8825, 11:30 A.M.–10 P.M. Mon.–Sat., US$5–18) has good dim sum every day. The shrimp dumplings are a favorite.

Canton Express Restaurant (43 St. James St., tel. 876/952-6173, 10:30 A.M.–7 P.M. Mon.–Sat., US$3.50–7.50) has roast chicken, oxtail, shrimp, chicken chow mein, and shrimp fried rice.

China House Restaurant (32 Gloucester Ave., tel. 876/979-0056, 10 A.M.–10 P.M. daily, US$2.25–22.50) serves Chinese, Mongolian, Thai, and Jamaican cuisine, as does its neighbor, **Golden Dynasty Chinese Restaurant** (39 Gloucester Ave., tel. 876/971-0459, 11 A.M.–10 P.M. Mon.–Sat., noon–10 P.M. Sun., US$2–20). China House serves dim sum on Sundays.

Chilitos (Shops #1 and #2, Doctors Cave Beach Hotel, Gloucester Ave., tel. 876/952-4615, 11 A.M.–10 P.M. Mon.–Sat., 1–10 P.M. Sun.) serves Jamexican specialties like quesadillas, tacos, and burritos, as well as mixed drinks and of course tequila, with a happy hour 5–7 P.M. on weekdays.

Akbar and Thai Cuisine (tel. 876/953-8240, Half Moon Shopping Village, noon–3:30 P.M. and 6–10:30 P.M. daily, US$10–24) is a decent, dependable Thai restaurant sharing a venue with a North Indian place. Staples like chicken or shrimp pad Thai on the Thai side complement items like chicken tikka masala and lobster bhuna from the Indian kitchen. This is Mobay's branch of the same restaurant found on Holborn Avenue in Kingston.

Fine Dining

◖ **The HouseBoat Grill** (Southern Cross Blvd., Freeport, tel. 876/979-8845, houseboat@cwjamaica.com, www.montego-bay-jamaica.com/houseboat/index.html, 6–11 P.M. Tues.–Sun., bar open from 4:30 P.M., happy hour 5:30–7 P.M., US$12–26) on Montego Bay's Marine Park is an unparalleled setting for a romantic dinner, and the food is excellent. Dishes include chicken, fish, and lobster.

MONTEGO BAY

© OLIVER HILL

You won't find a more picturesque setting for a romantic sunset dinner than at The HouseBoat Grill.

The HouseBoat Grill is run by Scott Stanley, and reservations are recommended.

The Groovy Grouper Bar & Grill (Doctors Cave Beach, tel. 876/952-8287, fax 876/940-3784, groovynews@islandentertainmentbrands.com, margaritavillecaribbean.com, 9:30 A.M.–10 P.M. daily, US$10–24) serves excellent food ranging from fish tea to steamed fish and bammy to steak and lobster tail. The setting on Doctors Cave Beach is unbeatable in Montego Bay and is popular with locals and tourists alike. The restaurant holds regular events like its seafood buffet every Friday (7–10 P.M., US$25) and full-moon party every three months (on select Saturdays).

The Twisted Kilt (tel. 876/952-9488, 11 A.M.–2 A.M. daily, US$8–25) is a sports bar that opened in 2008, offering "pub & grub." The pub has several big-screen TVs, free Wi-Fi, and a bar menu with wings, fries, fish and conch shamrocks, soups, salads, sandwiches, burgers, and entrées like fish and chips, steaks, pasta, and sautéed tofu. On Fridays, 2-for-1 martinis are on offer for the ladies 6–9 P.M. The bar

serves specialty drinks like the twisted mojito, Mackeson Stout, and Olde English Cider in addition to the typical bottled beers found widely in Jamaica.

The Native Restaurant (29 Gloucester Ave., tel. 876/979-2769, US$9–12) is easily one of Mobay's best, with an extensive menu including items like smoked marlin appetizer or Caesar salad with spicy shrimp and entrées like Yard Man steamed or escovitch fish or gingered plantain–stuffed chicken. Vegetarian options include garlic char-grilled vegetables and green vegetable coconut curry. The Boonoonoonos Native sampler platter is a good way to get a taste for a variety of Jamaican dishes in a single sitting. Other creations bring an international flair to traditional cuisine with dishes like ackee and saltfish quesadillas and lobster roll-ups. The restaurant's in-house band performs smooth, live dinner music Tuesday–Saturday. Dinner is served starting at 5:30 P.M., with the last order taken at 10:30 P.M. Families are always welcome, and reservations are strongly suggested. Free door-to-door transport is provided to many hotels and villas in the area.

Marguerite's (Gloucester Ave., adjacent to Margaritaville, tel. 876/952-4777, 6–10:30 P.M. daily, US$20–50) is the fine dining wing of Mobay's popular Margaritaville, serving dishes ranging from the Caribbean-style chicken to seafood penne and sugarcane-seared drunken lobster tail.

 Day-O Plantation (Fairfield Rd., tel. 876/952-1825, cell tel. 876/877-1884, dayorest@yahoo.com, www.dayorestaurant.com, US$16–35) was formerly part of the Fairfield Estate, which at one time encompassed much of Mobay. It is perhaps the most laid-back and classy place to enjoy a delicious dinner. Entrées range from typical chicken dishes to lobster. A beer costs US$3–5. Day-O is a favorite for weddings and other events that require the finest setting around a gorgeous pool. Owners Jennifer and Paul Hurlock are the most gracious hosts, and on a good day Paul will bring out his guitar and bless diners with his talent. Other professional musicians who have played at the restaurant's dinner shows include guitar legend Ernest Ranglin, jazz artist Martin Hand, and steel pan artist Othello Molineaux.

Pier 1 Restaurant and Marina (tel. 876/952-2452, 9 A.M.–11 P.M. daily, later on weekends) is an excellent restaurant and entertainment venue. The Sunday seafood buffet starting at 3 P.M. is a must. Pier 1 hosts a Pier Pressure party on Fridays, a fashion and talent show on Wednesdays, and occasional large events. The grounds just outside the restaurant are a venue for a few nights of Reggae Sumfest. Appetizers include crunchy conch (US$4.50), chicken wings (US$6.25), and shrimp cocktail (US$7.50), while entrées include chicken and mushrooms (US$10), bracelet steak (US$18), whole snapper (US$16/lb.), and lobster (US$28).

The Sugar Mill Restaurant (across the highway from Half Moon Shopping Village, tel. 876/953-2314 or 876/953-2228, 6–10 P.M. daily) is one of the area's high-end establishments, specializing in Caribbean fusion cuisine with openers like pumpkin or conch soup

(US$7.50), spring rolls, smoked marlin or conch in fritters, salad, or jerked (US$13–15). Entrées range from coconut-crusted or escovitch fish to lobster tail (US$35–50).

Norma's (Altamont West, tel. 876/620-4540, US$15–35) specializes in Caribbean fusion cuisine. Its founder, Norma Shirley, manages several restaurants under her name around the island. The food is on the pricey side and includes entrées like stuffed chicken breast, oxtail, curried goat with the chef's own mango chutney, lamb chops and lobster. Appetizers include ackee with salt fish, marlin salad, and crab back.

Sweets and Ice Cream

Calypso Gelato (Lot 9, Spring Garden Main Rd., Reading, tel. 876/979-9381, 8 A.M.–6 P.M. Mon.–Fri., 9 A.M.–6 P.M. Sat., 10 A.M.–6 P.M. Sun.) is the only producer of Italian gelato in Jamaica, with a small retail shop at its factory west of Montego Bay in Reading, just past the turnoff up Long Hill, next door to Ramson Wholesale. Calypso boasts more than 50 flavors of gelato, either milk or water-based, using local fruits. A cone or cup with two scoops costs US$2, medium cups are US$3.50, and large cups are US$5.

Tortuga (www.tortugarumcakes.com) located on the same compound, produces the Caribbean's most commercially successful rum cake and retails the cakes from the same shop.

Devon House I Scream (Bay West Center, tel. 876/940-4060) is open 11 A.M.–11 P.M. daily and has some of the best ice cream around.

INFORMATION AND SERVICES
Organized Tours

Most of the major organized tours to attractions across the island run out of Montego Bay and/or Negril, with transportation included as part of a package with entry fees and sometimes a meal. These include Mayfield Falls, Chukka Cove, Rhodes Hall, and Caliche White River Rafting. The farm and plantation tours operate similarly, including transport and food.

The best and most versatile tour operator running, with transport to even the most remote and unheard-of interesting corners of Jamaica, is **Barrett Adventures** (contact Carolyn Barrett, cell tel. 876/382-6384, info@barrettadventures.com, www.barrettadventures.com). With personalized service, Barrett Adventures tailors an excursion or even an entire vacation precisely to your interests and likings. Whether it's climbing Blue Mountain Peak, more humbly climbing Reach Falls in Portland, tubing down the YS River, or getting a historical tour of Falmouth, veteran adventurer Carolyn Barrett will get you there and ensure that anything you could want to do gets done in the allotted time-frame—which, if you're lucky, won't be less than a week.

Banks and Money

As elsewhere in Jamaica, the easiest way to get funds is from an ATM with your regular bankcard. Nevertheless, you can get slightly better rates in the cambios, or currency trading houses, that can be found all over town.

NCB has locations at 93 Barnett Street (tel. 876/952-6539), 41 St. James Street (tel. 876/952-6540), and Harbour Street (tel. 876/952-0077), with ATMs at Sangster Airport and at the junction of 92 Kent and Gloucester Avenues.

Scotiabank is at 6–7 Sam Sharpe Square (tel. 876/952-4440), 51 Barnett Street (tel. 876/952-5539), and Westgate shopping plaza (tel. 876/952-5545).

FX Trader is a an exchange house that gives the best rates around. FX has locations at Hometown FSC (19 Church), Medi Mart (Shop #1, St. James Place, Gloucester Ave.) and at Hometown Overton (Shop #9, Overton Plaza, Union St.).

Government Offices

Jamaica Tourist Board (18 Queens Drive, tel. 876/952-4425) has information about attractions in the region.

Internet Access

The best place in Mobay to get online if you have a laptop is **Richmond Hill**, where there is no charge to use the Wi-Fi, which reaches from the open-air lounge across the veranda and pool area. Richmond Hill has the best view of Mobay's harbor in town. Buy a drink from the bar or a snack in appreciation for the service. Otherwise the **Parish Library** (Fort St., tel. 876/952-4185, 9 A.M.–5 P.M. Mon.–Sat.) offers Internet access as well (US$1.50/hour.)

Computer World (13 Strand St., tel. 876/952-3464, fax 876/952-3464, cell tel. 876/538-9519, computerworld@cwjamaica.com or earljoel@yahoo.com, 10 A.M.–6:30 P.M. Mon.–Fri., 10 A.M.–7 P.M. Sat.) offers Internet, copies, and printing as well as making CD compilations. Internet rates run US$1.10 per half hour.

Medical Services

Mobay Hope Medical Center (Half Moon, Rose Hall, tel. 876/953-3981) is considered by many the best private hospital in Jamaica.

Soe-Htwe Medicare (14 Market St., tel. 876/979-3444) is the best private clinic in town.

Supermarkets

Adwa (West Gate Plaza) has a wide array of natural foodstuffs like imported organic grains as well as cosmetics products by Tom's of Maine.

Little Jack Horner Health Food Store (2 Barnett St., tel. 876/952-4952) has nice baked goods and pastries.

Parcel Services

Both **DHL** (34 Queens Dr., tel. 888/225-5345) and **FedEx** (Queens Dr., tel. 888/GO-FEDEX or 888/463-3339) have operations near the airport. Domestic carrier AirPak Express (tel. 876/952-8647) is located at the domestic airport terminal.

GETTING THERE AND AROUND
By Air

Donald Sangster International Airport (Jamaica Tourist Board information desk, tel. 876/952-2462, airport managers MBJ Ltd., tel. 876/952-3133) is the primary point of entry for most tourists visiting Jamaica. The airport is located by Flankers district a few minutes east of the Hip Strip and about 10 minutes from Downtown or from Rose Hall.

Beyond the national airline, Air Jamaica, Sangster airport is served by many North American and European carriers including US Airways, Delta, United, Air Canada, Northwest, American, Spirit, Continental, Cayman Airways, and Virgin. The domestic airline industry has been challenging historically, with little continuity of service among carriers and a slew of different domestic airlines coming and going over the years.

The domestic terminal is located separately from the international terminal. To get to the domestic terminal turn left from the main entrance just after coming off the roundabout, before reaching the gas station.

Skylan Airways (tel. 876/932-7102, reservations@skylanjamaica.com, www.skylanjamaica.com, office hours 8:30 A.M.–4:30 P.M. Mon.–Fri.) operates out of Norman Manley International Airport in Kingston with six weekly flights between the capital and Montego Bay (morning and afternoon departures Mon., Wed., Fri.). The morning flights depart Kingston at 7:30 A.M., with the return departing Mobay at 8:30 A.M.; afternoon flights depart Kingston at 4 P.M. with the return departing Montego Bay at 5 P.M. The trip lasts about half an hour and costs US$70 each leg. Skylan also offers charters when its aircraft is not in use on regularly scheduled flights. It operates a Jetstream 32 19-seater aircraft with a pressurized cabin.

Jamaica Air Shuttle (tel. 876/906-9025, 876/906-9026, or 876/906-9027, www.jamaicaairshuttle.com) is an affiliate of air cargo and courier companies Airways International and Airpak Express. It began offering regular flights between Kingston and Montego Bay in late 2009, departing from Tinson Pen Aerodrome with three Beach 99 Turbo Props seating 12 and one Queen Air with a five-person capacity. The carrier has 62 flights between Kingston and Mobay weekly Monday–Saturday (US$120 each way) and also offers charters.

International AirLink (tel. 876/940-6660, tel. 876/971-4601, or from U.S. tel. 954/241-3864, intlairlink01@gmail.com, res@intlairlink.com, www.intlairlink.com) offers charter service from Mobay to Kingston (US$134), Negril (US$134 for two persons), Boscobel, and Port Antonio ($1,575). Airlink passes on bank charges of an additional five percent when paying with a credit card.

Buses and Route Taxis

Buses and route taxis run between Mobay and virtually every other major town in the neighboring parishes, most notably Sav-la-Mar in Westmoreland, Hopewell in Hanover, Falmouth in Trelawny, and Runaway Bay in St. Ann. The bus terminal on Market Street is a dusty and bustling place where it pays to keep your sensibilities about you. Buses to any point on the island, including Kingston, never exceed US$7. Time schedules are not adhered to but you can generally count on a bus moving out to the main destinations at least every 45 minutes.

Real Deal Taxi Service and Tours (Curtis cell tel. 876/436-5727 or 876/971-8212) will take you wherever you want to go in a comfortable van holding up to eight passengers.

Car Rentals

Island Car Rentals (tel. 876/952-7225, icar@cwjamaica.com, 8:30 A.M.–10:00 P.M. daily) is Jamaica's largest and most dependable rental-car agency, aligned with Alamo, Enterprise, and National. It has an outlet in the international terminal at Donald Sangster International Airport. Island offers Toyota, Mitsubishi, Nissan, and Suzuki vehicles, with sedans, SUVs, and vans at competitive rates.

Central Rent-A-Car (Gloucester Ave., tel. 876/952-3347, or Sunset Ave., tel. 876/952-7485, toll-free tel. 800/486-2738) rents Mazda, Toyota, Nissan, and Honda sedans, plus Toyota and Mazda minibuses (US$90–115 daily).

Dhana Car Rental & Tours (4 Holiday Village Shopping Centre, tel. 876/953-9555) has vehicles ranging from Toyota Starlets to Toyota Noah minivans and gives heavy discounts on the walk-in weekly rates for reserving a month (US$75) or week (US$50) in advance.

Sunsational Car Rental & Tours (Suite #206, Chatwick Centre, 10 Queens Dr., tel. 876/952-1212, fax 876/952-5555, sensational@ cwjamaica.com, www.sensationalcarrentals. com) is located across from the airport and has decent rates on a variety of Japanese cars (from US$40/55 per day low/high season for a Corolla). The company also offers free cell phones with a minimum two-day rental. The minimum age is 21, with a young driver surcharge until age 25. Maximum age for drivers is 68.

Alex's Car Rental (1 Claude Clarke Ave., Karen Fletcher, tel. 876/940-6260 alexrental@ hotmail.com, www.alexrental.com) has 2001–2005 Corollas, Nissan Xtrail, Suzuki Vitara, and Honda CR-Vs (US$40/50 per day low/ high season plus tax and insurance).

Thrifty Car Rental (28 Queens Dr., tel. 876/952-1126, 7 A.M.–9 P.M. daily) has 2003 and 2004 Toyota Corollas (US$92 per day including insurance and tax).

Prospective Car Rentals (2 Federal Ave. at Hotel Montego, across from the airport, tel. 876/952-3524, fax 876/952-0112, reservations@jamaicacar.com, 8 A.M.–5 P.M. Mon.–Fri., till 4 P.M. Sat.) rents a 2004 Toyota Yaris, Nissan Sunny, Toyota Corolla, and RAV4 (US$45–85 per day plus tax and insurance).

ST. JAMES INTERIOR

The St. James Interior extends from the coast inland as far as the Trelawny border, where Cockpit Country begins. The interior can be accessed from Montego Bay along three main thoroughfares: One extends up Long Hill from Reading west of Mobay; the next heads inland from Catherine Hall along the continuation of Fairfield Road, ultimately skirting the western end of Cockpit Country leading into St. Elizabeth; and the third road heads inland due east into Trelawny along the northern flanks of Cockpit Country. This last road (B15) is an alternate scenic route leading to Windsor Caves, even if it does take a few extra hours due to the road's poor quality.

From the western side of town, Long Hill extends from Reading up along the Great River to where it meets the Westmoreland border. Developed tourist attractions in this area consist mainly of a few low-key river rafting operations, Rocklands Bird Sanctuary, and a few plantation tours.

Sights and Recreation

Caliche Rainforest Whitewater Rafting (tel. 876/940-1745 or 876/940-0163, calicheadventuretours@yahoo.com, www.whitewaterraftingmontegobay.com) is the only true whitewater-river rafting tour in Jamaica, based on the upper reaches of the Great River, which runs along the St. James–Hanover parish border. Rafting excursions (1.5–2 hrs.) depart daily at 10 A.M. and 1 P.M. (US$90 per person with transport from Negril or Mobay included). For those with their own transportation (deduct US$10), park at the Caliche office (first building on left above the post office at the base of Long Hill in Reading) and ride up with the group that was picked up from hotels in Mobay or Negril. Caliche also operates on the Rio Bueno in Trelawny. The location in Trelawny affords Class III rapids even during the dry season (Feb.–Apr.) when it's no longer possible to navigate the upper reaches of the Great River. A slower, Class I–II rafting ride (US$80 adults, US$60 children under 12) is geared toward children as well as adrenaline-shy adults. Caliche is an Arawak word meaning "river in the mountain."

Mountain Valley Rafting (Lethe, tel. 876/956-4920 or 876/956-4947, 8:30 A.M.–4:30 P.M. daily, US$45 per raft) operates bamboo pole rafts along the Great River for a meandering rather than thrilling ride. To reach the launch site, go up Long Hill, take the second right turn at Cross Roads at the small Les Supermarket, and continue nearly five kilometers from the intersection until you cross the bridge into Hanover. Pickups from hotels in Montego Bay are offered (US$20 per person), as is a tractor-drawn banana plantation tour (US$15).

Great River Rafting (US$20) is offered on long bamboo rafts along the lower reaches of the Great River and out onto the tranquil bay where it exits into the sea. Immediately after crossing the Great River, turn inland and back to the river's edge, where several rafts are tied up under the bridge. Ask for Hugh.

Rocklands Bird Sanctuary and Feeding Station (Anchovy, tel. 876/952-2009, noon–5:30 P.M. daily, US$10 per person) was created by the late Lisa Sammons, popularly known as "the bird lady," who died in 2000 at age 96. Sammons had a way with birds, to say the least, summoning them to daily feeding sessions even after going partially blind during the last years of her life. Since her death, the feeding sessions have been upheld and the sanctuary maintained by Fritz, his wife Cynthia, and their son Damian. Visitors are instructed to sit on the patio and hold hummingbird feeders, which entice the birds to come perch on their fingers. There is also a nature trail where the property's 17 species can be sighted. To get to Rocklands, head up Long Hill from Reading and turn left off the main road as indicated by a big green Rocklands Bird Sanctuary sign. Follow one abominable road to the top of the mountain and down the other side, about 100 meters, turning right at the first driveway on the downhill.

Rocklands Cottage (US$150–200 for up to six people) is a cute three-bedroom on the property that has one king-size bed, one queen-size bed, two twin beds, two bathrooms, and a kitchen with a big living and dining room. The cottage has air-conditioning and hot water.

Northern Cockpit Country

East of Montego Bay proper, Ironshore and Rose Hall cover the coast with hotels and housing developments that range from middle-class to super-luxury before reaching Greenwood, a small community once part of the Barrett estate that sits beside the sea, bordering the parish of Trelawny. The Trelawny coast has a smattering of tourism development concentrated in the area just east of Falmouth along the bay, while the inhabited parts of Trelawny's interior are covered in farming country, where yam, sugarcane, and citrus fruit are major crops. The early morning mist that rises from dew-covered cane fields makes a trip through the interior from Rock, Trelawny, to St. Ann a magical alternative to the coastal route at this time of day.

◖ FALMOUTH

Trelawny's capital, Falmouth, is today a run-down shadow of its short-lived former Georgian prime. Nevertheless, noble and much-appreciated efforts are under way to dust off years of neglect and shine favor on the town's glorious past by restoring its architectural gems. Falmouth was formed in 1790 when the port of the former capital Martha Brae silted up and shippers needed an export base. The town was laid out in a well-organized grid and named after Falmouth, England, birthplace of then-governor William Trelawny, who lent his name to the parish. The land for the town was acquired from Edward Barrett, who owned Greenwood Estate a few kilometers west. For the town's first 40 years during the height of Jamaica's sugar production, Falmouth experienced a housing boom and was fashionable amongst the island's planter class. But as the sugar industry faded in importance, so too did Falmouth, leaving a virtual ghost town by the late 1800s.

Today, with somewhat decent roads and its close proximity to resort areas in Montego Bay, the town is attracting a growing population once more. Thanks to the efforts of a nongovernmental organization (NGO) known as **Falmouth Heritage Renewal** (4 Lower Harbour St., tel. 876/617-1060, jmparrent@yahoo.com, www.falmouth-jamaica.org), the town has become a laboratory for architectural restoration. Falmouth Heritage Renewal, directed by James Parrent, has been working for several years to revitalize the architectural heritage of Jamaica's most impressive Georgian town by training local youth in restoration work. The Georgian Society in Kingston (tel. 876/754-5261) has a wealth of information on Falmouth.

Falmouth is famous for its **Bend Down Market,** held every Wednesday since the town's founding.

Sights

The **Baptist Manse** (Market St., cell tel. 876/617-1060) was originally constructed as the town's Masonic Temple in 1780. The building was sold in 1832 to the Baptist Missionary Society, which had lost many buildings in raids of terror and reprisal following the slave rebellion of 1831, in response to the Baptists' fiery abolitionist rhetoric. The building was home to several Baptist missionaries before it was destroyed by fire in the 1950s, to be reconstructed as the William Knibb School in 1961. Today the building serves as headquarters for the Falmouth Heritage Renewal.

Falmouth Courthouse was built in 1815 in classic Georgian style, destroyed by fire, and rebuilt in 1926. The building stands prominently on a little square facing the water just off the main square at the center of town.

Trelawny Parish Church of St. Peter the Apostle (Duke St.) is one of the most impressive Anglican structures in Jamaica, built in typical Georgian style. It was constructed in 1795 on land donated by rich estate owner Edward Barrett, whose descendent, Elizabeth Barrett Browning, would go on to become a well-recognized feminist poet of the Romantic movement. The parish church is the oldest public building in town and the oldest house of worship in the parish.

Other historic churches in Falmouth include the **Knibb Memorial Baptist Church** (King and George Sts.) named after abolitionist missionary William Knibb, who came to Jamaica in 1825 and established his first chapel on the site of the existing structure, which was erected in 1926, and the **Falmouth**

The restored Baptist Manse operates as headquarters for Falmouth Heritage Renewal, an NGO dedicated to the restoration of the town's architectural treasures.

© OLIVER HILL

Presbyterian Church (Rodney and Princess Sts.), which was built by the Scots of the parish in 1832. Knibb's first chapel was destroyed by the nonconformist militia after the Baptist War, a.k.a. Christmas Rebellion of 1831–832. Later structures were destroyed by hurricanes. A sculpture relief inside Knibb Memorial depicts a scene (repeated at several Baptist churches across the island) of a congregation of slaves awaiting the dawn that granted full freedom in 1838.

Falmouth All Age School sits on the waterfront in a historic building and makes a good destination for a stroll down Queens Street from the square.

Shopping

Falmouth is by no means a shopping destination. Nevertheless, there is a small mall on Water Square with a few crafts shops to poke around.

For more original crafts, call **Isha Tafara** (cell tel. 876/610-3292 or 876/377-0505), an artist and craft producer who lives in Wakefield near Falmouth, farther inland from Martha Brae. Tafara makes red, green, and gold crocheted hats, Egyptian-style crafts, handbags, belts, and jewelry with a lot of crochet and fabric-based items. Tafara works from home, which can be visited by appointment, and supplies Things Jamaican, among other retailers.

Services

Club Nazz Bar & Restaurant (23 Market St., tel. 876/617-5175, 7 a.m.–11:30 p.m. daily) offers customers free Wi-Fi.

For groceries and supplies, try **T&W Supermarket** by the Texaco station.

Next to the courthouse there's a **Scotiabank** branch built in replica Georgian style, with an ATM.

FX Trader (tel. 888/398-7233) has a branch at Big J's Supermarket on Lower Harbour Street (8:30 a.m.–4:30 p.m. Mon.–Wed. and Fri.–Sat., 8:30 a.m.–12:30 p.m. Thurs.).

Trelawny Parish Library (Rodney St., with entrance on Pitt St., tel. 876/954-3306, 9 a.m.–6 p.m. Mon.–Fri., till 4 p.m. Sat.) offers free DSL Internet.

The **Falmouth Police** are based along the waterfront on Rodney Street (tel. 876/954-5700).

MARTHA BRAE

The town of Martha Brae was Trelawny's first parish capital, before the mouth of the river silted up and forced the relocation of the port from Rock to Falmouth. Along with several other locations in Jamaica, Martha Brae is thought to have been the location of the first Spanish settlement of Melilla. Until 1790 when the first bridge was constructed across the river, a ferry was in service. Today, with the North Coast Highway, it's possible to speed past without noticing the river at all. Martha Brae is a literal backwater, with little to distract tourists as they pass through on their way to start the rafting trip or to Good Hope Plantation in the Queen of Spain Valley.

The **Martha Brae River** is one of Jamaica's longest rivers and is navigable for much of its 32 kilometers, extending to the deep interior of Trelawny, from where it wells up out of the earth at Windsor Cave. The river's name is an awkward derivation of Para Matar Tiburon Rio, which translates literally as "to kill shark river." Legends surround the Martha Brae, likely owing to its important role in the early colonial years, when the Spanish used the river to reach the North Coast from their major settlement of Oristan, around present-day Bluefields. The first commercial rafting tour began in 1970.

Just east of Martha Brae, straight inland from Falmouth, the **Greenfield Stadium** was built for the Caribbean's hosting of Cricket World Cup in 2007. The stadium is now used for sporting events and entertainment, becoming the venue for Jamaica Jazz and Blues Festival in 2010.

Martha Brae Rafting

Martha Brae Rafting (tel. 876/940-6398 or 876/940-7018 or 876/952-0889, info@jamaicarafting.com, www.jamaicarafting.com, 9 a.m.–4 p.m. daily) is the most developed bamboo rafting attraction in western Jamaica.

Rafts hold two passengers in addition to the raft man, who guides the vessel down the lazy Martha Brae. The tour (US$55) includes a welcome drink; round-trip transport can be arranged from Mobay (US$15 per person). To reach the departure point on the Martha Brae River, exit left off the highway ramp after passing the first turnoff for Falmouth heading east. Turn inland (right) through the underpass, continuing into the small village of Martha Brae. At the intersection in the town, turn left and then right after the second bridge. The five-kilometer raft ride takes about 90 minutes. The excursion will not get the adrenaline pumping, but it's a relaxing and romantic experience.

The Luminous Lagoon

The Luminous Lagoon is one of Jamaica's favorite natural phenomena, created from a unicellular dinoflagellate less than ⅟₅₀₀th of an inch in diameter, *Pyridium bahamense,* which glows when the water is agitated. The organism photosynthesizes sunlight using chlorophyll during the day and then emits the energy at night. Tours of the Luminous Lagoon are offered at **Glistening Waters Restaurant & Marina** (tel. 876/954-3229, info@glisteningwaters.com, www.glisteningwaters.com) and **Fisherman's Inn** (tel. 876/954-4078 or 876/954-3427, fishermansinn@cwjamaica.com). The Glistening Waters tour (US$17/person) lasts half an hour, with boats leaving the marina every half hour 7–9 P.M. nightly. Fisherman's Inn organizes virtually identical outings (US$15/person) every evening at 7 P.M.

Glistening Waters also offers fishing charters from the Marina (US$600) on a 46-foot sport fisher with a capacity of eight people. A smaller, 32-foot boat (US$400/four hours) carries five people. Two complimentary drinks per person are included on fishing excursions. The marina also welcomes visiting yachts (US$1/foot/day) and can accommodate boats of up to 86 feet. Boaters should call ahead for special instructions on entering the lagoon. Longer stays can be negotiated.

Montego Bay Jamaica Fishing Charter and **Luminous Lagoon Tours** (contact captain David Muschett, cell tel. 876/995-9885, awahoo2@yahoo.com), based at Fisherman's Inn on the Luminous Lagoon, is a one-stop-shop for deep-sea fishing, night excursions on the lagoon, and a variety of water sports activities from parasailing to scuba diving, water skiing, and snorkeling aboard a 38-foot Bertram with an eight-person capacity. Fishing trips chase marlin, kingfish, barracuda, sailfish, wahoo, and a host of other species. Rates range from US$550 for a half day with up to four passengers to US$1,000 for eight hours with up to four passengers, including bait and tackle. Add US$35 per extra person. Paintball and ATV tours are also offered by David Muschett in the Martha Brae vicinity.

Accommodations

Queen of Spain Villa (Irwin Towers Estate, Martha Brae, contact Michele Lawrence, cell tel. 876/877-6959, michelelawrence1@yahoo.com, US$40–60 per night) has a total of five rooms available for rent in an owner-managed villa along the Martha Brae River. Three rooms have queen-size beds, and one has two single beds, with a king-size bed in the master room. Wi-Fi and continental breakfast are complimentary. There's a pool on the one-acre property and the river is also suitable for swimming.

Fisherman's Inn (tel. 876/954-4078 or 876/954-3427, fishermansinn@cwjamaica.com, from US$75) is a hotel and restaurant on the Luminous Lagoon with clean, spacious rooms overlooking the lagoon and a small marina with private baths and hot water, TV, and either fans or air-conditioning. Jean Lewis is the very helpful and accommodating manager.

The inn organizes outings every evening (US$15 per person) at 7 P.M. on the lagoon to see the phosphorescent microbes light up the agitated water.

Time 'N' Place (adjacent to Pebbles, call owner Tony Moncrieffe, tel. 876/954-4371, cell tel. 876/843-3625, timenplace@cwjamaica.com, www.mytimenplace.com) is the quintessential laid-back rustic beach spot with an open-air seafood restaurant and beach bar and four cottages planted in the sand (US$80–100). The spot has been a local favorite since it opened in 1988. The cottages are comfortably rustic, with front porches, basic foam queen-size beds, fans or air-conditioning, Jamaican art on the walls, and private bathrooms sectioned off with hot water. Tony offers coffee, fruit, and toast for breakfast. The restaurant (8 A.M.–8 P.M. daily) prepares excellent seafood and Jamaican favorites including jerk chicken, coconut shrimp, and grilled lobster, as well as burgers and fries. Wi-Fi covers the entire property.

FDR Pebbles (next to Time 'N' Place along the old main road, tel. 876/973-5657 or 876/617-2500, US$250) bills itself as an eco-friendly, family-oriented resort. The hotel is by no means exemplary in the environmental department, however, with clear signs of dumping of gray water into the bay and a generally untidy backyard. Pebbles, along with its sister property in Runaway Bay, has created the family-friendly niche by proving nannies for guests. Pebbles' private beach has been sectioned off from the expanse with a pair of stone piers. Nevertheless, guests often hop the fence to get a taste for the authentic Jamaica vibe found next door at Time 'N' Place. All rooms at Pebbles have air-conditioning, ceiling fans, and hot water.

Excellence Resorts (www.excellence-resorts.com) is building a 450-room, adults-only, luxury all-inclusive resort on five kilometers of beach adjacent to Time 'N' Place. Construction began in 2007 but completion was delayed when the global economy fell into recession in 2009.

Food

(Club Nazz Bar & Restaurant (23 Market St., tel. 876/617-5175, or contact manager Carlton Cole, cell tel. 876/475-7125, 7 A.M.–11:30 P.M. daily, US$4–25) serves good seafood and Jamaican staple dishes and offers customers free Wi-Fi. The food is excellent and a good value. The Upa Level Culture Bar

& Grill on the third floor serves food from the same kitchen with a view over town.

Located on the second level, **Club Nazz** opens Tuesdays–Sundays, from 6 P.M. until you say when, playing mostly reggae, dancehall, R&B, and hip-hop. A jazz bar and lounge is located downstairs in the basement.

In the center of Falmouth on the square there is a small Juici Patties kiosk, as well as **Spicy Nice** (Water Square, tel. 876/954-3197), a bakery that sells patties, breads, pastries, and other baked goods.

Three roads lead off the North Coast Highway into Falmouth, one from the east, where the old highway used to run, the other, Market Street, a straight shot to Martha Brae, and the third, Rodney Street or Foreshore Road, to the west toward Mobay. Along the easternmost road, two restaurants sit adjacent to one another on the Luminous Lagoon in Rock district.

Fisherman's Inn (tel. 876/954-4078, fishermansinn@cwjamaica.com) is a hotel and restaurant facing the lagoon. The restaurant serves items like callaloo-stuffed chicken breast, stuffed jerk chicken, lobster, and surf and turf (US$13–30).

Glistening Waters Restaurant & Marina (tel. 876/954-3229, info@glisteningwaters.com, www.glisteningwaters.com) has food ranging from oyster bay seafood chowder (US$4) to the Falmouth Seafood Platter (US$35), which comes with grilled lobster, shrimp, and snapper.

(Aunt Gloria's (Rock district, cell tel. 876/353-1301, 6 A.M.–8:30 P.M. Mon.–Sat., US$3–4.50) serves brown stew fish, fried chicken, curry goat, and brown stew pork. Gloria opens her jerk center on Fridays and sometimes on Saturdays for the best jerk pork and chicken in town. Breakfast items include ackee and saltfish, kidney, dumpling, yam, and banana.

Along the same road toward Falmouth, a jerk center keeps irregular hours, mostly opening on weekends.

Culture Restaurant (Foreshore Road, contact proprietor Pablo Plummer, cell tel. 876/362-4495, 8 A.M.–8 P.M. daily, US$4–8)

offers a decidedly Rasta experience and takes the cake for original roots value. It's a small restaurant and cultural center where Ital food and juices are served in an atmosphere brimming with black pride and Rastafarian symbolism. Owner Pablo Plummer is as conscious as they come and also incidentally runs independent PADI diving courses with full equipment provided, after spending years as a dive instructor at a number of resorts along the North Coast.

EAST OF FALMOUTH
Sights

Outameni Experience (Coopers Pen opposite Breezes Trelawny, tel. 876/954-4035, cell tel. 876/836-6725 or 876/409-6108, info@outameni.com, www.outameni.com, US$36 adults, US$18 children under 12) is a cultural attraction that takes visitors through Jamaica's history into modern times, from the Taino to Rastafarians. The 90-minute tour, set on a five-acre property, touches on Jamaica's art, music, theater, and dance traditions. A fun

village offers children games and a water slide at an additional cost of US$3.

Duncans

A small community on a hillside overlooking the sea, Duncans has little to interest visitors in the town itself. Just below the population center, however, the coast is lined with fine, white sand, split between two spectacular beaches: Jacob Taylor Public Bathing Beach, and **Silver Sands Beach** along the waterfront at the gated community of Silver Sands, comprising cottages and villas. Silver Sands charges US$15 per person for day use of the beach and facilities. There's a restaurant and bar and small grocery store, the Villa Mart, at the complex. It's necessary to call ahead (tel. 876/954-2518) to gain access to Silver Sands so they expect you at the gate.

About a kilometer east of Silver Sands, a private estate house lies in ruins facing a small beach, also with fine white sand and crystal waters. To get there, turn off the main road down to Silver Sands through a green gate and

© OLIVER HILL

Sea grapes grow along Harmony Cove, a pristine beach near Duncans destined for a major hotel and casino development.

drive along a rough, sandy road pocked with coral through the scrub forest until reaching the coast again.

A 20-minute walk farther east along low coral bluffs leads to **Mango Point,** where one of Jamaica's few remaining virgin beaches is found. Known as **Harmony Cove,** the area is to be the site of a massive resort development planned for the coming years, with several hotels and casinos envisaged, pending a change in Jamaica's law to allow gambling of this sort. Harmony Cove can also be reached by turning off the North Coast Highway next to a cell phone tower coming from the east; from there, drive toward the coast along a dirt road and turn off along a sandy track that disintegrates at the water's edge. Park and rejoin the road on the other side of the fence, walking the remaining distance. It's about 20 minutes' walk from the east as well. Contact Harmonisation (876/954-2518) for more information on the status of the resort development.

Silver Sands

Silver Sands (www.mysilversands.com) is a gated community of 44 rental cottages and villas that range considerably in their level of price and comfort, from rustic to opulent. Even at the higher end of the price range, Silver Sands villas are among the best value for your money to be found in Jamaica, on what is considered by many the island's finest beach.

Queen's Cottage (US$275/325 nightly, US$1925/2275 weekly low/high season) is named after the cottage's most illustrious guest, Queen Elizabeth II, who stayed there on a trip to Jamaica, and located directly on the waterfront. It is a three-bedroom villa with a king-size bed in the master, one queen-size bed in the second bedroom and two twins in the third, making it ideal for families or a small group of friends. Bedrooms have ceiling fans, air-conditioning, and private bathrooms. A large wood deck overlooks the sea a few steps off the beach. The villa boasts a large Jacuzzi and is the closest of any at Silver Sands to the water's edge.

Windjammer (tel. 876/929-2378 or 876/926-0931, dianas@cwjamaica.com or

© OLIVER HILL

Silver Sands is a small villa community on the Trelawny coast ideal for family getaways.

MONTEGO BAY

bookings@windjammerjamaica.com, www.windjammerjamaica.com, US$457/557 nightly, US$3,200/3,900 weekly low/high season) is an impeccably furnished four-bedroom luxury villa with a private pool, DSL Internet, a large veranda with sea view, and a built-in barbecue. Two bedrooms have king-size beds, one has a queen, and the fourth has two twins.

Jacob Taylor Bathing Beach

Located across the compound walls from the gated community at Silver Sands, Jacob Taylor Bathing Beach is a local hot spot where low-key craft vendors sell their goods and anglers park their canoes to while away the days playing dominoes in the shade. The beach itself extends for a few kilometers to the west, and while not immaculately swept and maintained daily like Silver Sands, the sand is fine, the water's clear, and there's no entry fee. You can't miss the entrance to Jacob Taylor Bathing Beach, marked by a large sign by the road that leads downhill toward the sea to the left of the gated entrance to Silver Sands.

Accommodations

The Sober Robin Inn (tel. 876/954-2202, soberrobin@gmail.com, US$35 d) is a no-frills accommodation opened in 1979 that rents nine rooms, each with one double or two single beds, air-conditioning, and cable TV. The inn was under expansion in 2010, with additional rooms under construction for a projected total of 23. The inn was once owned by the grandparents of Harry Belafonte, who is said to have spent his childhood there. It is located just past the Silver Sands turnoff heading west out of Duncans, or on the right just after leaving the highway on your way into Duncans from the west.

Sea Rhythm (Jacob Taylor Bathing Beach, contact caretaker Cardella Gilzine, cell tel. 876/857-0119, US$200) is a three-bedroom cottage a few steps from the shore. The master bedroom has a king-size bed and air-conditioning, with a double bed and fan in the second room and two twins in the third. Each room has a private bath with hot water, and there's a fully equipped kitchen. Meals are prepared to order.

Food

Leroy's (cell tel. 876/447-2896, US$3–12) is a local bar and restaurant, located seaside at Jacob Taylor Fisherman's Beach that serves fish and Jamaican staples. Leroy can usually be found in the kitchen, and his step daughter, Cameika "Chin" Wallace, works the bar. The Silver Lights Band performs live reggae on Saturdays starting at 8 P.M. late into the night. The no-frills restaurant and bar is notable for its relaxing atmosphere that draws a healthy mix of locals and tourists, appreciably devoid of hustlers to interrupt the quiet seaside landscape.

GREENWOOD

Natural Vibes Gift Shop Bar & Restaurant (Long Bay, Greenwood, tel. 876/953-1833, 8 A.M.–10:30 P.M. daily) has a mix of seafood and Jamaican favorites like curry lobster (US$25), curry shrimp (US$20), escovitch fish (US$15), jerk chicken (US$10), and jerk pork (US$12–13). The waterfront property is a favorite chill-out spot for Montegonians and tourists alike.

Father Bull Bar, Jerk Centre and Restaurant (Greenwood, cell tel. 876/422-3011, 8 A.M. until you say when daily) specializes in jerk chicken and pork, roast fish, seafood, and Jamaican staples, accompanied by breadfruit.

Far Out Fish Hut and Beer Joint (Greenwood, contact owner Ian Dalley, cell tel. 876/954-7155 or 876/816-6376, 10 A.M.–10:30 P.M.) serves steamed and roast fish, conch, octopus, and escovitch grilled conch, accompanied by bammy or bread.

Johnnie Reid's Paradise Grill & Restaurant (contact Johnnie Reid, cell tel. 876/863-4659, 10 A.M.–close), located in Salt Marsh between Greenwood and Martha Brae, serves Jamaican staples, seafood, and conch (US$5–8), as well as fish and lobster priced according to weight.

COCKPIT COUNTRY

Some of the most gorgeous and unexplored countryside in Jamaica lies in the interior of Trelawny, where Cockpit Country, with its myriad caves, sinkholes, and springs, stretches from the St. James border in the west to St. Ann at the heart of the island. Hiking and exploring in this region is unparalleled, but adequate supplies and a good guide are essential. Meanwhile, the Queen of Spain Valley, only a few minutes' drive inland, is one of the most lush and picturesque farming zones in Jamaica, where the morning mist lifts to reveal stunning countryside of magical, lush pitted hills.

Cockpit Country has some of the most unusual landscape on earth, where porous limestone geology created what is known as Karst topography, molded by water and the weathering of time. Cockpit Country extends all the way to Accompong, St. Elizabeth, to the south and Albert Town, Trelawny, to the east. Similar topography continues over the inhospitable interior as far as Cave Valley, St. Ann, even farther east.

There are three principal routes leading into Trelawny's interior and providing access to the northern border of the impassible Cockpit Country. The first few routes lead inland from Martha Brae. To get to Good Hope Plantation, bypass the town of Martha Brae to the right when heading inland from the highway, and take a left less than 1.5 kilometers past the town, following well-marked signs. Continuing on the road past the turnoff to Good Hope ultimately leads to Wakefield, where the B15 heads back west to Montego Bay.

By taking a left at the stop sign in Martha Brae, and then a right after crossing the river, the road leads inland past Perth, Reserve, and Sherwood Content, to where it ultimately peters out near Windsor Caves.

◖ Queen of Spain Valley

Good Hope Plantation (cell tel. 876/469-3443, goodhope1@cwjamaica.com, www.goodhopejamaica.com) located in the Queen of Spain Valley, is one of the most picturesque working estates on the island. Citrus has today replaced the cane of the past, while the plantation's great house and a collection of its historic buildings have been converted into the

the Great House at Good Hope Plantation in the Queen of Spain Valley

© OLIVER HILL

MONTEGO BAY

MONTEGO BAY

most luxurious countryside villas, with a total of 10 bedrooms between the main house, the carriage house, and the river cottage (rates starting at US$3,500/4,400 weekly low/high season for 3BR River Cottage). Good Hope features old-world luxury that sets itself apart from any other accommodation option on the island, with authentic antique furniture decorating every room, while not skipping the modern luxuries like iPods and air-conditioning. The villas are fully staffed with the most professional chefs, housekeepers, and gardeners to be found anywhere.

Good Hope is the ideal place for family retreats, birding, hiking, and mountain biking. There is no better place for horseback riding, which is still the best means of exploring the surrounding countryside. Of course, the inviting swimming pools and a brimming river make relaxation a favorite pastime for guests as well. Good Hope is rented through the owners.

David Pinto's Ceramic Studio (8 km north of Falmouth, cell tel. 876/886-2866, dpinto@cwjamaica.com, www.jamaicaclay. com, 8 A.M.–4 P.M. Mon.–Fri. or by appointment) is run by a Jamaican-born potter who studied ceramics during high school in the United Kingdom and later at Rhode Island School of Design before practicing in New York City. He returned to Jamaica in 1992 to establish his present studio in the Queen of Spain Valley on Good Hope Plantation, where he runs retreats led by internationally acclaimed guest master potters. Pinto's work includes both functional and decorative pieces and is on display in the permanent collection at the National Gallery in Kingston. A stop by Pinto's bustling studio with its five kilns is a great excuse to visit the spectacular grounds of Good Hope, a working citrus plantation.

Albert Town

A small hamlet at the edge of Cockpit Country, Albert Town is the center of Trelawny's yam-growing region, which celebrates the crop each year with the **Trelawny**

Yam Festival. Albert Town is the base for the **South Trelawny Environmental Agency (STEA)** (tel. 876/610-0818, www.stea.net), which organizes the yam festival and also offers guided excursions with its **Cockpit Country Adventure Tours** outfit in the surrounding area. They offer four different tours that cover caving and hiking. STEA is one of the best-organized environmental advocacy organizations in the country.

Windsor

Located at the farthest accessible point into Cockpit Country, Windsor is a small community. **Windsor Great Caves** is its main draw. Franklyn (Dango) Taylor is the sanctioned warden for the Jamaica Conservation and Development Trust (JCDT) and the official guide for Windsor Great Caves. The caves are best visited with Dango (US$20), though experienced cavers may prefer to go it alone. All visitors should check in with Dango, and sign the guestbook at the very least, which serves to both monitor efforts and provide some degree of accountability in the case of emergencies. Dango runs a little shop selling drinks and snacks. The source of the Martha Brae River is located nearby, affording a great spot to cool off.

The Windsor Caves are rich in both geological history and animal life, with up to 11 bat species emerging to feed in the evenings in large swarms. The geological formations should not be touched inside the caves, and a minimal-impact policy should be generally observed, which starts with visitors staying on the established path. Shining flashlights on the ceiling is also not advisable, since it disturbs the resting bats. Michael Schwartz, of Windsor Great House located nearby, warns of a chronic respiratory ailment caused by a fungus that grows on bat dung, afflicting cavers.

For more in-depth spelunking of lesser-known attractions, **Jamaica Caves Organization (JCO)** (info@jamaicancaves. org, www.jamaicancaves.org) is a useful group that knows Cockpit Country literally inside and out. It can arrange guides for hiking as well as caving. There is also a good circuit mapped out on its website to take a driving tour of Cockpit Country for those not interested in exercise. For those with a serious interest in hiking, the **Troy Trail** is one of the most interesting and arduous hikes in western Jamaica, traversing Cockpit Country from Windsor to Troy. Again, the JCO can provide guides and maps for a reasonable fee that goes toward helping to maintain the organization.

Accommodations
The Last Resort (Ivor Conolley tel. 876/931-6070, cell tel. 876/700-7128, iscapc@cwjamaica.com) is the most remote accommodation option in Cockpit Country. It's the headquarters for Jamaica Caves Organization, led by chairman Stefan Stewart. The facilities were recently renovated but remain rustic with 20 bunk beds (US$15 per person) and a common bath. One private room has a queen-size bed. Expect intimacy with the surrounding environment—bug repellent is an essential item.

Windsor Great House (cell tel. 876/997-3832, windsor@cwjamaica.com, www.cockpitcountry.com) was built by John Tharp in 1795 to oversee his vast cattle estate, which included most of the land bordering the Martha Brae River. Today the great house is operated by Michael Schwartz and Susan Koenig, who offer rustic accommodation and a weekly "Meet the Scientists" dinner (US$25 for the dinner).

Getting There
To get to Windsor, head inland from Falmouth to Martha Brae, crossing the bridge to the east and turning right to follow the valley south into the hills. On the way, the road passes through the small farming communities of Perth Town and Reserve. Once the road leaves the riverbanks, it heads to Sherwood Content, Coxheath, and finally Windsor. To get to Last Resort, turn right at Dango's shop, continuing for about 1.6

kilometers; a left at Dango's shop leads to Windsor Great House. A vehicle with good clearance is recommended, but the route is traveled frequently by vehicles with low clearance, driven with caution.

BURWOOD BEACH
The small community neighboring SuperClubs Breezes Trelawny has the spectacular Burwood Beach in Bounty Bay, which is also called Mutiny Bay. It's the best spot in Jamaica for **windsurfing** and **kite surfing** thanks to its gradual slope and lack of reefs that make these sports perilous in most other areas of the island. Brian Schurton runs **Brian's Windsurfing and Kitesurfing** (cell tel. 876/586-0900 or 541/490-2047, bws@gorge.net) with an informal windsurfing and kite-surfing school and rental outfit on the beach. With essential equipment like harnesses lacking in most of the all-inclusive resorts, windsurfers will find more professional gear at Brian's. Rates run US$160 for a 2.5-hour kitesurfing lesson. Windsurfing is US$60/day for gear, US$70 for a two-hour lesson. To get there, turn off the highway toward the sea about 1.5 kilometers east of Breezes Trelawny next to a sign for Bounty Bay.

Accommodations
Breezes Trelawny (Coopers Pen, Falmouth on Burwood Beach, tel. 876/954-2450 or U.S. tel. 800/GO-SUPER (800/467-8737), www.superclubs.com, US$99/139 per person low/high season) is the place to go if you love water slides, video gaming, trapeze acrobatics, and water sports. Rooms come with a stocked fridge, TV, air-conditioning, and CD player, but with all the activities in store, you won't be there much. Starfish is the SuperClubs brand's most budget-friendly and family-oriented property.

Breezes Rio Bueno (tel. 876/954-0000 or U.S. tel. 800/GO-SUPER (800/467-8737), glbreservations@superclubs.com, www.superclubs.com, US$224/349 per person low/high season) is the second all-inclusive in Jamaica, centered on a re-created and much-tamer-than-typical Jamaican village courtyard area, where dinners are served under the stars. Rooms are luxurious by American standards, with spacious suites that have balconies and large sitting areas. All the amenities of home are there, and the fridge is stocked daily with beer and soft drinks. Breezes has a decent beach and large swimming pool areas with the best food of the SuperClubs properties and premium liquors. The hotel sits on a 34-hectare estate. Horseback riding and tennis are some of the more popular activities at the resort, while water sports like scuba, snorkeling, and sailing are also offered.

Braco Stables (tel. 876/954-0185, bracostables@cwjamaica.com, www.bracostables.com, US$70 with transportation from Mobay or Runaway Bay, US$60 without transport) offers very tame horseback riding tours where riders traverse the Braco estate in single file. Experienced riders may be disappointed, as there is little freedom to roam about and leaving the group is not an option.

RIO BUENO

The first community in Trelawny across the border from St. Ann, Rio Bueno is considered by many experts to have been the actual landing point for Christopher Columbus on his second voyage, while that claim is also made for Discovery Bay. The port at Rio Bueno was an important export point, as can still be seen by the dilapidated warehouses and wharves along the waterfront beside the community's only accommodation, the **Rio Bueno Hotel.**

The small village is today undergoing somewhat of a renewal, with the new North Coast Highway bypassing the town entirely, which could ultimately enhance its picturesque appeal even while the busy Rio Braco rest stop will be less relevant.

The riverbank along the Rio Bueno is great for a stroll; visitors can see ruins of the **Baptist**

Theological College. The college was the first of its kind in the hemisphere. Other ruins in town include those of **Fort Dundas** behind the school. The **Rio Bueno Baptist Church** was originally built in 1832 before being destroyed by the Colonial Church Union, whose mostly Anglican members organized militias to terrorize the abolitionist Baptists, who were upsetting the status quo. The church was quickly rebuilt twice as large in 1834, and the present structure was built in 1901. While the roof is largely missing, services are still held downstairs.

The **Rio Bueno Anglican Chuch** was built at the water's edge in 1833 and remains there today. The church was petitioned by the community after years of attending service in a rented space.

The extensive **Gallery Joe James,** on the grounds of the Lobster Bowl and Rio Bueno Hotel, displays artwork by proprietor Joe James, among other selected Jamaican artists. The gallery extends throughout the restaurant, bar, and hotel and makes for a surreal waterfront setting. The restaurant itself is enormous, with outside seating extending out on a dock along the waterfront, as well as inside a large dining hall.

The Rio Bueno Primary School up the road is sometimes used for entertainment and events.

Accommodations and Food

Rio Bueno Hotel (tel. 876/954-0048, galleryjoejames40@hotmail.com, US$100) is a 20-room rustic accommodation with balconies overlooking the sea, ceiling fans, TV, and hot water in private baths. The ground floor rooms are larger and geared toward families, with three double beds.

The Lobster Bowl Restaurant (tel. 876/954-0048, 8 A.M.–10 P.M. daily, US$18–40) serves excellent shrimp, chicken, fish, and lobster. The restaurant was founded by Joe James and his wife, Joyce Burke James, over 40 years ago.

www.moon.com

DESTINATIONS | ACTIVITIES | BLOGS | MAPS | BOOKS

MOON.COM is ready to help plan your next trip! Filled with fresh trip ideas and strategies, author interviews, informative travel blogs, a detailed map library, and descriptions of all the Moon guidebooks, Moon.com is all you need to get out and explore the world—or even places in your own backyard. While at Moon.com, sign up for our monthly e-newsletter for updates on new releases, travel tips, and expert advice from our on-the-go Moon authors. As always, when you travel with Moon, expect an experience that is uncommon and truly unique.

MOON IS ON FACEBOOK—BECOME A FAN!
JOIN THE MOON PHOTO GROUP ON FLICKR

MAP SYMBOLS

▦ Expressway	☾ Highlight	✗ Airfield	⚲ Golf Course
⋯ Primary Road	○ City/Town	✗ Airport	ⓟ Parking Area
— Secondary Road	◉ State Capital	▲ Mountain	▰ Archaeological Site
⬚ Unpaved Road	◉ National Capital	✛ Unique Natural Feature	⛪ Church
- - - - Trail	★ Point of Interest		
⋯⋯ Ferry	• Accommodation	⚐ Waterfall	⛽ Gas Station
⋙ Railroad	▼ Restaurant/Bar	▲ Park	◯ Glacier
▦ Pedestrian Walkway	▪ Other Location	◩ Trailhead	◩ Mangrove
⫶ Stairs	⋀ Campground	⛷ Skiing Area	▨ Reef
			▱ Swamp

CONVERSION TABLES

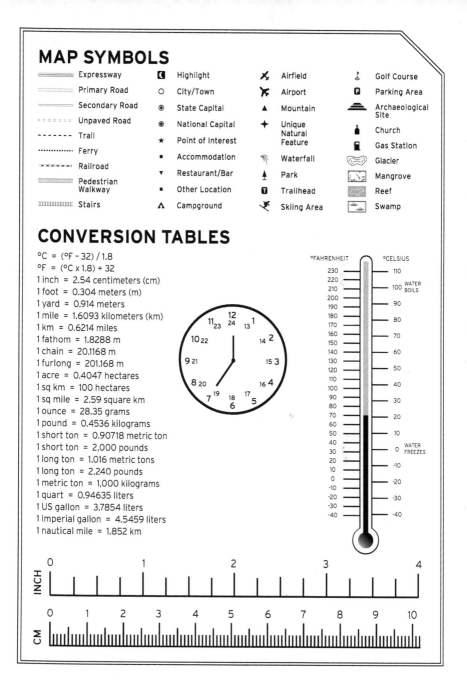

°C = (°F – 32) / 1.8
°F = (°C x 1.8) + 32
1 inch = 2.54 centimeters (cm)
1 foot = 0.304 meters (m)
1 yard = 0.914 meters
1 mile = 1.6093 kilometers (km)
1 km = 0.6214 miles
1 fathom = 1.8288 m
1 chain = 20.1168 m
1 furlong = 201.168 m
1 acre = 0.4047 hectares
1 sq km = 100 hectares
1 sq mile = 2.59 square km
1 ounce = 28.35 grams
1 pound = 0.4536 kilograms
1 short ton = 0.90718 metric ton
1 short ton = 2,000 pounds
1 long ton = 1.016 metric tons
1 long ton = 2,240 pounds
1 metric ton = 1,000 kilograms
1 quart = 0.94635 liters
1 US gallon = 3.7854 liters
1 Imperial gallon = 4.5459 liters
1 nautical mile = 1.852 km

MOON SPOTLIGHT NEGRIL & MONTEGO BAY

Avalon Travel
a member of the Perseus Books Group
1700 Fourth Street
Berkeley, CA 94710, USA
www.moon.com

Editor: Elizabeth Hollis Hansen
Series Manager: Kathryn Ettinger
Copy Editor: Valerie Sellers Blanton
Graphics Coordinator: Tabitha Lahr
Production Coordinator: Tabitha Lahr
Cover Designer: Tabitha Lahr
Map Editor: Brice Ticen
Cartographers: Chris Markiewicz, Kat Bennett
and Allison Rawley

ISBN-13: 978-1-59880-671-7

Some photos and illustrations are used by permission and are the property of the original copyright owners.

Front cover photo: Seven Mile Beach © Chee-Onn Leong/123rf.com
Title page photo: one of many gazebos at Sandals Montego Bay © Oliver Hill

Printed in the United States

ABOUT THE AUTHOR

© OLIVER HILL

Oliver Hill

A dedicated reggae fan from a young age, Oliver began his lasting relationship with Jamaica like many Americans – through the island's music. Friendships with fellow students of Jamaican heritage in high school ultimately led Oliver to visit the island, where he established a recording studio in a Kingston suburb in partnership with a local artist. Frequent trips to Spain and other destinations throughout his youth gave Oliver a global perspective on life and an unquenchable thirst for experiencing new places and cultures.

Later, a masters program in journalism at Columbia University took Oliver back to Jamaica with a film crew to shoot *Coping with Babylon*, a chronicle of contemporary Rastafarian philosophy that has appeared in international film festivals around the world and as part of an exhibition at the Smithsonian titled "Discovering Rastafari."

Oliver has worked as a video editor, ornithologist, and financial writer, and currently works as a correspondent for mergermarket, a Financial Times Group publication, in Latin America.

For more information on Oliver's film production company, check out www.sonerito.com. Visit his website, www.moonjamaica.com, for links to recommended lodging and services and up-to-date events coverage in Jamaica.